SOLA!

What are we fighting for?

Heather Choate Davis
Leann Luchinger

ICKTANK
PRESS

The Scripture references in this book are taken from either the ESV,
NIV, or NRSV translations unless otherwise noted.

Cover design: Heather & Lon Davis

Copy Editor: Christie Hutchins

ISBN: 978-0-9907642-6-7

TABLE OF CONTENTS

HOW WE CAME TO WRITE
THIS LITTLE BOOK

In the fall of 2011, Heather Choate Davis and Leann Luchinger arrived in the M.A. Theology program at Concordia University Irvine. They had never met but their stories were curiously similar: both were successful professionals in writing and communication fields, both put their kids into Lutheran elementary schools, came to faith as a result, and hungered to grow in the knowledge of His word. Throughout the M.A. program, they continued to marvel over the richness of theology—and just how few of the overarching insights ever made it to the pews. "Someone needs to tell people this stuff!" they would often proclaim. To which the professors would reply, "That's going to be your job."

Their first co-authored book was *Loaded Words*™, which is now used for group study and sermon series in LCMS and other churches all over the U.S. After a *Loaded Words* presentation at Concordia Seminary in St. Louis in 2016, they were invited back for the 500th Anniversary Theological Symposium and given the option of any Reformation topic. They chose the *solas*, not because they know so much more about them than the other fine scholars in attendance, but because they know firsthand how little the people in the pews understand them. Heather and Leann believe that one of their gifts to the church is helping pastors, teachers, and lay leaders reclaim and communicate these essential truths and their historical and eternal implications. *Soli Deo Gloria.*

We dedicate this book to
Dr. Charles Arand
who fights daily to open
minds, hearts, and doors.

"Infighting" from *The Art of Boxing and Science of Self-Defense*,
William Edwards, 1888, Excelsior Publishing House, NYC

What's a *sola?*

You don't need to know a lot about boxing to enjoy movies like *Raging Bull, Million Dollar Baby,* or *Rocky.* Even people who consider themselves true boxing fans— attending live events or paying steep prices for pay-per-view—can get what they want from the sport without having any knowledge of its ancient roots, its tumultuous history, the insider battles over rules and rule breakers, the pendulum swings in popularity, the way it's come to be organized and systematized, and the ongoing forces to eliminate the sport entirely. The people who stop by to watch a championship bout on a friend's new 72-inch flat screen can jump right in and pick someone to root for (maybe by their catchy nickname or the color of their shorts) without having any idea that there are immutable truths at play—e.g., that boxers have one of three distinct styles and (much like in rock, paper, scissors) each style has a clear advantage over one and a disadvantage against the other. These truths inform every step and jab and retreat of the combatants but whether or not you actually know any of this does not prevent you from playing the role of spectator.

But Christianity is not a spectator sport. While the undergirding truths of the faith are taught well to theologians and seminarians and the handful of believers who pursue them, they are rarely spoken of directly in a church service or even a Bible study. In this way, church is an unusual classroom. Students come and go, or come and stay forever. The message is taught through music and readings and preaching that endeavor to make the words of the Bible come alive in a personal way for a hundred—or a thousand—different people all at the same time.

The chronology moves in a continuous loop from Christmas to Easter and back again, stirring our hearts anew with memories of manger scenes and lily-covered altars from years past. In between those peak holy days, you might learn about things like Lent and Pentecost and the Transfiguration, and grow comfortable greeting fellow congregants with the peace of the Lord, even if that moment has no more deep theological meaning to you than a heartfelt hello and the growing sense that you belong.

In truth, you don't need to know a lot about Christianity to gain wisdom or solace or encouragement from a church service. Most would probably like to have a clearer sense of how all the dots of Bible verses and beliefs connect but the people responsible for teaching you—who would love nothing more than to answer all your questions if only they knew what they were—are likely unaware of what it is you don't understand. And you probably can't help them because you don't know exactly what it is you don't get. Or the question you really want to ask seems like it would leave you so exposed that you decide it's just not worth the risk.

Part of the disconnect is rooted in the fact that many church workers come from church worker families and learn the foundations of Christian doctrine along with shoe tying and *righty-tighty, lefty-loosey*. Even if they do not come from a church family background, by the time they've completed their formal theological education, they have heard the term "what we believe" so many times they assume that everyone already knows and believes these things. (We don't). These doctrinal principles are, for them, so deeply ingrained they imagine that the specifics of their weekly message carry with them a clear teaching on these core tenets, as well. (Not even close).

Any twenty-first-century middle school student googling the Reformation for a history paper could tell you that *sola* is Latin for *alone*, and that *the three solas* are considered foundational principles of Protestantism, brought into the world through the prophetic call of Martin Luther in 1517. But ask current members of a Lutheran church about the *solas* and be prepared to discover that most have never even heard of them. This is true not only of adult converts or of those in churches with more informal, outreach-friendly practices. In a 2017 mission workshop for lay people, a 70-year-old German-American man who had spent his whole life in an LCMS Lutheran church heard the term for the first time. Refusing to let his pride get in the way, he dared to ask what others in the room would not. "What's a sola?"

We can't know what we're not taught. Which is why over the course of this book, you will learn about the three *solas: sola gratia* (grace alone), *sola fide*[1] (faith alone), and *sola scriptura* (Scripture alone*)*. You will learn how they came to be, why they are essential, and what they were created to fight against. You will learn why they still matter today not only to the Church but to you, and to how you live out your faith. In learning this, you will be asked to open your eyes (briefly) to the glorious history of ecumenical debate and the inglorious legacy of political infighting in God's church, and how words or deeds that seemed at a given moment in time to be of critical and eternal importance have been both a blessing and a curse to us all.

Let's begin.

"I don't understand"

From the moment Jesus's name was first spoken, human beings have struggled mightily to reconcile who He was with their own existing worldview. It began with Mary, whom, upon hearing from the angel Gabriel that she was

---

[1] At different times since the Reformation both *fide* and *fides* have been used.

to give birth to the Son of the Most High, replied, "how can this be?"[2] Mary was experiencing what we today call cognitive dissonance, in this case between the divine mystery of Jesus and the limitations of her own understanding.

Twelve years later, when Jesus broke away from his family and friends to be with the great teachers at the temple in Jerusalem, the young boy's answers to their questions left them all "amazed."[3] By the time he began his earthly ministry two decades later, the mounting crowds were "astounded at his teaching, for he taught them as one having authority, and not as their scribes."[4]

Anytime we're presented with an idea, a possibility, a new reality that up until that moment we have never even considered, it challenges us to let go of an old, often contradictory belief—even as that old perspective fights mightily to retain its hold on us. This is why, day after day, the disciples had to fight their dull and hardened hearts to see what Jesus was trying to show them. And why, day after day, he would say to them, "Do you still not understand?"[5]

We often respond with violence to things we don't understand or which threaten our treasured stability. It should come as no surprise then, that the very crowds that had flocked to Jesus for healing and miracles (which they received in droves) had now grown fearful of his

---

2 Luke 1:34
3 Luke 2:47
4 Matthew 7:28
5 Cf. Matthew 16:9; Mark 8:17,21; Mark 9:32.

power. With no evidence of wrongdoing whatsoever, they shouted ever louder, "Crucify him!" So they did.

The victory was not at all what they had expected, taking the form of an empty tomb and leaving a small group of followers to make sense—risen how? risen where? risen why?—of a world that had just changed forever because of Him. Many of them were Gentiles, who had come to believe that Jesus had died "once for all," now including them in the family of God. Many of God's first chosen people had become believers, too, yet they were still deeply rooted in the Law of Moses. Feeling that they had "met the Gospel halfway" by accepting Jesus as the promised Messiah, they asserted that these Gentiles must submit to their traditions as well. "Unless you are circumcised according to the custom of Moses, you cannot be saved."[6]

The conflict reached a fever pitch at a gathering in Jerusalem.[7] A compromise was impossible because there is no such thing as being "a little bit circumcised." Had the decision been left to nothing more than the preferences and temperaments of men, the Jewish and Gentile converts would most likely have split then and there, effectively destroying the Church while it was still in start-up mode. Instead, faced with the option of saying, "I'm outta here," or "please, Lord, help me understand," they listened to the Spirit of God who allowed them to respond favorably to Peter's words:

---

[6] Acts 15:1

[7] This gathering is considered the first ecumenical council and is referred to as the Jerusalem Council.

God, who knows the human heart, testified to them by giving them the Holy Spirit, just as he did to us; and in cleansing their hearts by faith he has made no distinction between them and us. Now therefore why are you putting God to the test by placing on the neck of the disciples a yoke that neither our ancestors nor we have been able to bear?[8]

The good fight

Getting a group of people to agree on anything of real importance is no small feat. A unifying center needs to be defined as well as the concentric circles of acceptable variation. When individuals test the bounds of even those wide margins, the group must decide whether their mutual understanding of who they are and what they do as a group has been so thoroughly breached that their shared center point can no longer hold them all.

If, for example, a group of people decide to make up a sport where two men hit each other until one admits he can't go on, they will need to ask themselves (as they did in the Ancient world) if it changes the nature of their shared vision of "boxing" if one of them wraps his hands in strips of soft suede for protection; or if the other wraps his hands in hard, rough-edged leather intended not to protect but to further brutalize. And if each of these slight variations is okay, then how about if one of them

---

[8] Acts 15:8-10

embeds a sharp barb under the leather, effectively changing the endgame from defeat to death. Are these two men still involved in the same sport? If not, what should be done about it?

Now imagine you're a Christian in the first centuries of this new faith. What exactly is the center point? Was it Jesus's teaching? His miracles? Or was the entire message of God's radical and almost incomprehensible new covenant with the world somehow embedded in His body on the Cross? While the first Christian martyrs were making the stakes of this game-changing battle of beliefs clear, others were quietly laboring to find the words to express truths that transcend human understanding.

For the first three hundred years, the external forces of persecution (by Roman authorities who demanded fidelity and taxes, as well as by Jewish authorities who rejected the claim that Jesus was the long-prophesied Messiah) were matched by an equal level of zeal and confidence among believers. Then in a blink, everything changed. Many say it was due to a divine vision or the influence of his mother; others contend it was nothing more than political opportunism. The heart of a man is knowable only to God but these facts are certain: in the early decades of the fourth century, Constantine, the emperor of Rome, began to look with considerable favor on the Christian faith and it quickly went from being an oppressed cult to the *de facto* official religion of the state. This ended much of the persecution, yes, but also brought with it the jockeying for power and proximity to power that comes with every human system on earth.

Throughout Constantine's reign, beautiful and terrible things happened in the name of Jesus. Free from the burdens of persecutions, many early believers shifted their energies away from preaching the Gospel and began sparring with one another over the nuances of theology. Among these battles were questions about the Holy Spirit and how best to define the relationship between the three names of the Trinity. For many this fight for truth and clarity was their gift to the Church for all time. For others it was blood sport. From Rome to the eastern regions of Syria, Egypt, and East Africa, theological skirmishes erupted. Seeing the need for unity, Constantine called the first ecumenical (all members as one) council in Nicaea in 325 AD.

At that time the Church was called The Great Church, both catholic[9] and orthodox[10] and it was broken into five regions.[11] Four were Eastern (Alexandria, Constantinople, Antioch, Jerusalem) which were made up predominantly of black and brown members. One was Western, predominantly white, and centered in Rome. Representing these five sees, some 318 bishops and elders convened. Ragged from the journey, and many scarred or disfigured from the tortures of persecution, they threw themselves into rigorous debate over the core tenets of our faith, providing checks and balances for one another, and holding steadfast to the essential biblical principle that God longed for them to remain as One. A certain

---

[9] Universal
[10] True teaching
[11] Called sees (pronounced says)

faction made the case that any decrees should be crafted solely from scriptural wording, while another saw this as a trap. Even in the fourth century people were "cherry picking" verses to try to win the day!

As a result of this good fight, which lasted over fifty years and two councils, they created what is now called the Nicene Creed. From that day forward, the term *heresy* (a self-chosen opinion) was applied to representations of the Gospel that were not consistent with this ecumenical agreement. This very human document, created through an arduous and spiritual process by disparate people with a common love of Jesus Christ, was further evidence of the Holy Spirit taming the discordant hearts of men. In doing so, the Spirit of the Living God gave all believers for all time a place to point as their true north of Christian identity.[12]

Irreconcilable differences

It's often the little things that lead to our undoing. At some point in the sixth century—likely at a local synod meeting in Toledo, Spain—someone said, "don't you think it would be better if the Creed said that the Holy Spirit proceeds, "from the Father *and the Son,*" not just "from the Father?" Next thing we know this revision begins appearing in all sorts of worship services throughout the Western Christian world. No one seemed

---

[12] See page 118 for the Nicene Creed.

to question the change or to check in with the Eastern churches to see what they thought of it. Many in Europe preferred the slight elevation of Jesus over the Holy Spirit. By the time leaders from the East got wind of the revision, the altered Creed had been in use for several hundred years.

To the Eastern fathers, this small change (referred to as the *filioque*) was not small at all because it subordinated the Holy Spirit, who they viewed as the Giver of new life itself. Which side was right about the hierarchy of the Trinity? Hard to say. Scripture can be used to support either point of view. The real problem was much deeper than revisions; it was the fact that those additional words violated an *ecumenical* agreement—a sacred allegiance between brothers in Christ—and, in doing so, created an irreversible breach of unity and trust.

The damage was done. And there was no clear path forward because the Eastern and Western branches of The Great Church, both catholic and orthodox, were no longer in agreement about who had the final say. So it was, roughly a thousand years after Jesus changed the salvation story of the world, that the East broke from the West, the darker from the lighter, the "Eastern Orthodox" from the new "Roman Catholic," and the Body of Christ endured its first corporal dismembering.[13]

---

[13] To this day, each tradition considers itself to be the continuation of the church of the apostles that was born on the day of Pentecost (Acts 2); and that *they* are the true holy, catholic, and orthodox church.

Martin Luther and the solas

Another five hundred years would pass before the second major disembodiment of the Church, set in motion by Martin Luther and the period of change called the Reformation. Luther was a young monk in the Augustinian tradition of the Roman Catholic Church. His interior life was under siege as a deep and relentless spirit of unworthiness and despair seemed the only possible response to the imperious and oppressive portrayal of God in his day. Then he got hold of the New Testament in its original Greek language, and life as he knew it would never be the same. Where the sixteenth-century Church of Rome taught that God's approval was a reward he should spend every waking moment trying to earn, the Living God revealed through Scripture something else entirely: that we don't need to earn His love at all. We never did. And we never will.[14]

These first glimmers would lead to the systematic truths we now call the *solas*. They were not some lofty academic teaching, but rather, the weapons God had given Luther to fight for the restoration of the "bride of Christ"—the Church—which had become little more than a shell of pageantry: spiritually apathetic and wholly corrupt. Scripture was not taught and rarely referred to. When it was it was in Latin, and not a single soul outside the clergy understood a word of it. Had a worshipper wanted to ask a priest a question about Jesus's life or

---

[14] Luther's journey of understanding likely began with his lectures on Romans in 1515/16; Romans 1:17 the key verse.

teaching, they would have been told it was not something they needed to know—and then handed an offering plate.

When Luther posted his now infamous 95 theses on the church door at Wittenberg, his intent was simply to call out the errors for discussion. He was certain that Pope Leo would commend him for his vigilance and hurry to remedy the problems. Instead, the Pope—who was shepherding a number of significant capital campaigns that guilt, fear, and the inviolability of clerical authority were funding nicely—declared that Luther must be drunk (curious, as this is what the people said of the apostles as they received the Holy Spirit on Pentecost[15]). Luther was then branded a heretic, a "wild boar in the vineyard of the Lord,"[16] and within a few years, was excommunicated.

The fighting—over doctrine and practice and what the word of God does and doesn't say—has been going on ever since. Fighting for the truth. Fighting against heresy. And sometimes just fighting because that's what men do. Yet, through it all, the simplicity and truth of *the three solas* remain, as potent and life-giving today as they were in 1517. [17]

---

[15] Acts 2:13

[16] From Psalm 80:12-13, quoted in the [Papal] Bull of Excommunication.

[17] The "three solas" did not actually appear as a systemized catchphrase until 1916, in a 400th Reformation anniversary article by Prof. Engelder. Since then, others have added *Solus Christus* (Christ Alone) and *Soli Deo Gloria* (To God Alone be the Glory) resulting in what some call the *five solae.*

For further discussion

1. Can you think of something (perhaps from religion, science, medicine) that you don't completely understand – but accept anyway?

   a. Is there a biblical or theological question you would like to ask a pastor or theologian, but are afraid or embarrassed to ask? Write it down here. Consider sharing with your small group or asking your pastor later.

2. READ Genesis 17:1-14. This section of scripture details an important covenantal relationship. In the Genesis reading: What does God promise Abraham? (Notice in vv.1-8 the number of commitments from God). What does God expect in response? How long does this covenant last (see. v.13)? What does this tell us about the relationship between circumcision and the covenant?

   a. READ Acts 15:1-19. Picture yourself as one of the apostles and elders (known as the Jerusalem Council). Why would you be concerned with circumcision? Would it be easy to let go of this rite?

b. Are you aware of conflicts or changes in your own church that may be of great importance. How do these types of things normally get resolved?

3. Have you ever heard of the Nicene Creed? Do you recite it in your church? The Nicene Creed is included on p. 118 for your reference.

   a. Page 9-10 gives a brief overview of the work to create the Nicene Creed. Was there anything that surprised you about this process or the people involved? Did anything give you comfort or conviction?

   b. On page 10 the word *heresy* is defined. What does this imply about the importance of the Nicene Creed?

4. On pages 10-11 you learned about the *filioque*.

   a. If you were part of the Eastern churches, how would you react to this change?

b. Now put yourself in the place of the Western Church, which has now been using the revised creed for hundreds of years. How would you respond?

c. Today we have a saying, "it's easier to ask for forgiveness than permission." Does that seem to apply here? What is at the heart of this philosophy?

5. Have you ever heard of the *solas?* How did you learn about them? Briefly share a little about how you learned about them and what you know.

Grace *alone*

Roberto Duran, inarguably one of the greatest boxers of all time, dared to say aloud what most of us secretly believe. "I'm not God, but I'm something similar." He had every reason to make the claim: in a sport that often chews people up and spits them out, he continued to win in ever more difficult and weightier divisions over the course of five decades. By any standard his was a glorious career. Although very few of us possess international titles in our chosen fields, the spirit with which we move through our days echoes Duran's worldview. "There may be some other divine kind of god, but as far as my to-do list, my bank account, my image, and my accomplishments go, I'm it."

This is our default setting. This is the right that we cling to with existential fervor. This is the part of the human condition that causes us, and everyone around us, harm. Even after we come to faith and start telling ourselves that God is in charge, this voice returns to us daily claiming that, in fact, *we* are the god of our lives. Or at least something similar.

This prideful insistence is the very essence of sin. Did you feel yourself wince at the sound of that word? Of course you did. We all do. Because the word *sin* threatens the view we love to have of ourselves as "good." Someone who is "entitled" or "deserving" or, in a world of seven-plus billion people, "special." Any reminder of the inescapable reality that we are not gods who reign but rather creatures who sin will sting: that's the plan. Because sin must be sin for grace to be grace.

Try to remember that the next time you hear the phrase "poor, miserable sinner," and find yourself swatting it away like some annoying relic of a bygone era. The endgame of facing our own sinful natures is not to make us feel bad (at least not for any more than a pin prick) but to create an entry point for God's redeeming truth. "If we say we have no sin, we deceive ourselves, and the truth is not in us."[1] Which means that grace is not in us.

Instead, we are likely living under a delusion of God as the keeper of the great sticker chart in the sky, and as long as He holds the chart and regularly acknowledges us on it, we're happy to let Him play His small role in our lives. What is that voice? Sin. And what do we know about sin? Without it there is no grace. So no, we can't just make an end run around sin and take the grace. Sin and grace are conjoined twins.

---

[1] 1 John 1:8

We humans don't like that—not one bit. Even if we've managed to brush up against the truth of our own sin in a moment of weakness (perhaps while listening to Aretha belt out *Amazing Grace* in an amphitheater in the dark), we are always quick to return to our default setting, filing *grace* back up on the shelf with the happy words like peace, love, and joy. Grace like icing. Like sprinkles. Like some shiny, happy God-glow that surely we deserve. Haven't we been to church three Sundays in a row? Didn't we bring a dish—not just a salad but a main course—to the last potluck? This notion of grace is what is called the Theology of Glory.

Theology of Glory

Simply put, it's what happens when "the church exchanges God-given grace for human religiosity: a jury-rigged system for appeasing the divine."[2] Though it's taken on different forms and movements over the years—and rears its ugly head in different ways and seasons in every church—it's always rooted in the same sin: the belief that we can negotiate the terms and conditions of our relationship with God.

Why is this such an easy sin to fall prey to? Well, for starters, the part of us that wants to be our own god doesn't like feeling like some charity case. We don't want to feel beholden to the Giver, and we certainly don't want the same gift that absolutely anyone can have. Nope.

---

[2] Vanhoozer, 40.

We'd rather operate within a system where the rules are clear, we can control them, and there's plenty of opportunity for advancement. So, thanks but no thanks, God. You can keep your free gift: we'd rather earn it. We'll pay and pray and abide by the rules and then believe that you must actually love us (and why wouldn't you?). And we'll gladly support the churches that allow us to believe this.

Well, wait a minute. This Theology of Glory doesn't sound all bad. It encourages people to participate and to see the church and their role in it as valuable. The name would surely test well in focus groups, and with the trouble we're having getting people to come to church these days, well, even if the motivation is a little off, the same good end is achieved, right?

This is the great lie of the Theology of Glory. It sounds so close to the right idea that we can't tell the difference. Not at first. Its message is so appealing because it uses our pride to convince us that grace is the way God rewards our moral striving. It reinforces our sense of self-righteousness with thoroughly unbiblical teachings like "God helps those who help themselves,"[3] and convinces us not to worry about our sins because there's plenty that we can do to make up for them. If you are part of a church held captive by the Theology of Glory you will surely believe that your faith life will lead to glorious things, unaware (or perhaps preferring not to see) that it's keeping you just on the other side of God's

---

[3] This popular "Christian" saying does not exist in Scripture: it is from a speech by seventeenth-century English politician, Algernon Sidney.

love, and unable to escape the corrosive cycle of self-doubt and longing and despair. *Am I really a good person? Have I done enough to prove it? Since my life isn't really that glorious, does that mean I'm doing something wrong—or God's a liar? Or He doesn't exist at all? Maybe if I just…*

The apostle Paul nailed the interior monologue of this timeless hamster wheel nearly two thousand years ago, "I do not understand my own actions. For I do not do what I want, but I do the very thing I hate…Wretched man that I am! Who will rescue me from this body of death?"[4]

These were the thoughts that tormented Luther's soul. This was the awakening that led him to see that what he'd been taught by the Church about "grace" was actually a trap, one from which he feared there was no escape. Then in the midst of his suffering, the Word began to dance and sing and call him back to the Spirit of the original voice, and his clenched fists softened and the good of the Good News rang true once more: Jesus is God's *gift* to the world. We don't need to train for it. We don't need to go 10 rounds without faltering. We don't even have to suit up because the decision is already in and Grace is holding our gloved hands up high, declaring us right with God. It's done. It's finished. We are good enough for God because God is more than good enough for us.

Once Luther saw this clearly there was no turning back. This is what led him to cry out *sola gratia*! Not grace *plus* works or worthiness or effort or intention or money

---

[4] Romans 7:15, 24

or remorse. *Grace alone!* "Grace will not be halved nor quartered, but receives us wholly and completely into favor."[5] It is an all or nothing proposition, with God doing all, and us doing nothing.

But why is it so important for God to feel like He's doing everything? If He were really so gracious, wouldn't He give us some credit for all the good things we're doing too? Believe it or not, the reason He takes all the credit is, actually, a favor to us, though it usually takes a while to understand why. When we do—when we begin to hear and learn about grace as a gift we do not deserve (stop saying that!)—the Holy Spirit will begin to reveal to us, just as He did to Luther, that whenever we allow even a sliver of our own efforts or worthiness to enter into the equation of grace, our sinful natures will glom right on. Given a foothold, our spiritual alter egos will then set up shop and begin bartering and rationalizing. And it's all downhill from there. This slippery misrepresentation of grace is the path away from Jesus and towards "our idolatrous preference for one's own thoughts about God."[6] With so many churches to choose from today, we can always find one that tells us what we want to hear.

Here's the thing we tend to forget: Jesus didn't come to fill churches. He came to heal the hearts and minds of His children, to model for us the "love that cares and stoops and rescues,"[7] and through that divine model, to give us lives of glorious fullness that extend out through

---

[5] Engelder, 108.
[6] Vanhoozer, 42.
[7] Stott, 214.

time and space eternally. This was the grace God revealed to Luther, and it was the most radical and disruptive reversal of thinking in the history of Christianity:

> Luther's discovery was not only new, it was unheard of: it rent the very fabric of Christian ethics. Reward and merit, so long undisputed as the basic motivation for all human action, were robbed of their efficacy. Good works, which church doctrine maintained as indispensable, were deprived of their basis in Scripture.[8]

Of course, this radical, disruptive thinking wasn't new at all. It was the message of the Cross. It was the Gospel that the first believers would have heard and embodied and shared. It was an utter rejection of the idea of buying or earning or choosing God's favor. It was the final word on the matter of grace: "It is finished."[9]

Theology of the Cross

How is it that a life of joy and purpose and meaning begins at a place of such wretchedness and suffering? Because the Cross of Christ is where sin and grace kiss. Not just once but daily. Remember where this chapter began? We talked about how our default setting is to believe "it's all on us." When our lives are going pretty well that means we get to tell ourselves that *we* made it happen (as opposed to God making it happen through

---

[8] Oberman, 154.
[9] John 19:30

and for us). If we don't have a means to recognize this for the lie that it is, we will continue further down that road of glory until we hit a speed bump: an illness, a job loss, a cycle of anxiety from which no amount of medication can save us, and suddenly our warped belief that "it's all on me," goes from parade banner to crushing burden. Can you see now why it's a trap?

When we meet grace at the Cross, our default setting becomes trust. Trust in God. Trust that He is already well acquainted with whatever pain or sorrow we're in. Trust that there will be redemption in the suffering. We can trust this because it was in and through suffering that we were joined to Him: sin to grace, pain to redemption, imperfect man to perfect God, death to resurrection.[10]

Where the Theology of Glory promises nothing but blue skies, the Cross tells us the truth: "in this world you will have trouble. But take heart! I have overcome the world."[11] That is to say, God tells it to us straight. Life is hard. There will be suffering. Sometimes we'll come to understand it (how often is the very joy or fullness we seek just on the other side of pain we'd do anything to avoid?). Sometimes our suffering will remain incomprehensible. But our lack of understanding can never change this fact: He is with us, helping us to carry the load, to put one foot in front of the other on a path that points always to hope.

---

[10] "We were therefore buried with him through baptism into death in order that, just as Christ was raised from the dead through the glory of the Father, we too may live a new life. For if we have been united with him in a death like his, we will certainly also be united with him in a resurrection like his" (Romans 6:4-5).
[11] John 16:33

Telling the suffering soul who's been groomed in glory thinking to just keep their eyes on Jesus can easily be heard as, "it's on you to get Jesus to get you out of this." This can set off yet another cycle of despair, pushing us further away from the mercy of God and, often times, from faith itself. After all, it's hard to smile and shout "Hallelujah!" when your heart is broken and the message that seems to be whispered just below the surface of all this talk about grace is that somehow it's all your fault. Although "the church is where salvation should be on conspicuous display,"[12] these very human systems often foster a culture that leaves people isolated in their greatest time of need.

> Once, I was at a party...This was at a time when it seemed like I had everything. I was young. I was undefeated. I had money. I'd just moved into my own home. People at the party were laughing and having fun. And I missed my mother. I felt so lonely. I remember asking myself, "Why isn't my mother here? Why are all these people around me? I don't want these people around me." I looked out the window and started crying. —Oscar De La Hoya

Most of our earthly days are not filled with triumph or tragedy, but rather with quiet joys and sorrows that may well be invisible, even to family and friends. This is the part of us that the Living God knows intimately, receiving us weary and broken, walking with us through our pain and confusion, restoring us to gratitude and hope. He

---

[12] Vanhoozer, 60.

demonstrates this grace again and again through the Cross until we know it even beyond our doubts. *Suffering redeemed. Life where there is no life. Life in all its fullness.*

Athletes call this muscle memory. It's the way our bodies make responses automatic and then build on them through repetition. For the boxer, the speed bag is the fount. For the believer it's the Cross, where God uses our sin and sorrow in all its manifold forms to extend goodness, kindness, and mercy freely and without condition—again and again and again and again. And again.

Okay, but how does the fact that Jesus died on a cross two thousand years ago really have anything to do with me or my "so-called" sins today? Well, think of it this way: we hate to admit the hard truths about ourselves. Most of us will do anything not to have to face our own weakness or meanness or loneliness or selfishness or how our actions have hurt other people. We prefer to deny or justify these parts of ourselves or keep them buried in some dark corner where they fester and swell. In that dark place they can never be healed, and the sickness they breed in our spirits leads us further away from the happiness we seek.

Then suddenly we're presented with the Gospel which promises us that we will not be shamed or scolded or punished or shunned but instead flooded with His love if only we allow Him to hold up a mirror to see that we are not, in fact, God. In that seismic moment the Holy Spirit opens the floodgates, takes our heart in His hands, and gives us the courage to face ourselves as we really are. Why does He do it? So "you will know the truth, and the truth will set you free."[13]

This is the epiphany. The truth we don't want to hear is not at all what we thought. God does not call us back to Himself because He loves authority but because He loves freedom. And us. What He's trying to tell us is that the very freedom of heart, mind, and spirit each one of us seeks is just on the other side of the Cross where suddenly the Word, "I am the way and the truth and the life"[14] sheds the stench of religious turf wars and opens, at long last, the doors to peace.

In the Lutheran tradition, the muscle memory of this grace is developed through a lens theologians call Law & Gospel. His Law (God's wisdom for living) reveals our sin (all the ways we reject that wisdom). His Gospel then assures us that we are not to sit around beating ourselves up about it but rather to keep following Him, trusting that "for freedom Christ has set us free."[15] Every Lutheran pastor is trained to give his sermon based on a Law & Gospel template but you could easily sit in a Lutheran church your whole life and not know that. The teaching is just beneath the words, but its presence (or absence) makes the difference between knowing that God is in charge or thinking that you are. Between knowing His grace is free or believing you have to earn it. A life-giving message will lead us to see that "we are more sinful

---

[13] John 8:32
[14] John 14:6
[15] Galatians 5:1

and flawed in ourselves than we ever dared believe, yet at the very same time we are more loved and accepted in Jesus Christ than we ever dared hope."[16] This balanced tension between Law & Gospel serves us in every season, keeping us humble through the highs, hopeful through the lows, and trusting that it's all on Him, regardless.

This Law & Gospel lens also reminds us that we're going to keep on being sinful even after we've received God's grace. Which means we should not expect perfect behavior from other Christians any more than they should expect perfect behavior from us. Even if we nod and claim we understand, we will still tend to imagine that our little "lapses" are nothing compared to the egregious offenses of others.[17] But, over time, as we are empowered by compassion to face our own failings, we will tend to grow in grace toward the shortcomings of others. In His time, we will begin to recognize that others are just living out a different flavor of sin than we are, and each of us is trapped in the same both/and reality. Luther called this simultaneously sinner and saved,[18] meaning none of us is pure sinner *or* saint, but both at the same time.

Why would God leave us sinful once we believe in Him and go to church and read the Bible and whatever else we're supposed to do? (There's that voice again). Well, let's think about what we've learned: it's the reminder of our sin that keeps us mindful that God is

---

[16] Keller, *The Meaning of Marriage.*

[17] Matthew 7:3 "Why do you look at the speck of sawdust in your brother's eye and pay no attention to the plank in your own eye?" In context cf. Matthew 7:1-5.

[18] Luther referred to this by the Latin phrase, *simul iustus et peccator,* simultaneously justified and sinner. Mueller, 300.

God. Without that reminder (which His Law provides) we will quickly return to believing that we are. If there were some sort of scale of improvement by which to measure our progress of sinlessness, that would just put us back into striving mode. Even though that's where we'd rather be, God knows we can never find peace there. So, in the face of our willful, prideful natures—which despise the idea of being weak or dependent—He leaves us with this assurance:

"My grace is sufficient for you, for my power is made perfect in weakness."[19]

Or, as Johnny Cash wryly put it: "My arms are too short to box with God."

---

[19] 2 Corinthians 12:9

For further discussion

1. Sin. This little word brings up all sorts of thoughts and images in people's minds. What do you think of when you hear the word *sin*?

2. On page 18 the authors suggest that pride is the essence of sin. C.S. Lewis writes that "there is no fault which makes a [person] more unpopular, and no fault which we are more unconscious of in ourselves. And the more we have it ourselves the more we dislike it in others."

    a. Have you ever heard the idea that pride is the essence of sin? Do you think this is accurate? Why?

    b. Does this differ from your own description of *sin* in question 1 above?

    c. Think about the sins you find most unpleasant, aggravating, annoying, or unforgiveable in others. Have you ever considered this may be God's way of holding up a mirror to reflect these very same sins in you?

3. READ Matthew 7:1-5. Do you see this behavior in your own life or in the greater society around you? How can you combat this tendency (that we all have)?

4. On pages 20-21, the authors offer a very human, very personal monologue about the struggle to find redemption. READ Romans 7:18-24. The Apostle Paul wrote this about his very human struggle. Can you relate?

    a. Martin Luther said we are all simultaneously sinner and saved. READ Romans 5:6-8 and John 3:16-17. How do these scriptures connect to Luther's assertion?

    b. How do the above verses from Romans 5 and John 3 help answer Paul's struggle and cry for help in the Romans 7 verses?

5. Law & Gospel. One way to understand God's Law is through what theologians call the *Three Uses* of the Law: 1) a curb, providing order in the world; 2) a mirror, like our conscience, showing us our sins; and 3) a guide, teaching us how to grow as people of God.

The Gospel, on the other hand, is entirely God's salvation work for us. Earned by God, through the death of His Son, and given to us—as a gift—no strings attached.

In the verses below, mark which are Law (can you tell which use?) or Gospel.

Exodus 20:2	
Leviticus 19:2	
Isaiah 53:5	
Matthew 20:28	
Matthew 22:36-39	
John 3:16-17	
Romans 2:15	
Romans 7:7-8	

6. In your own words, describe the difference between Theology of Glory and Theology of the Cross.

Faith *alone*

Redemption is one of the underlying themes of every great boxing movie, with *Rocky*—both the character and the franchise—the most iconic of them all. Four sequels in, our hero is still willing to risk his life in a David and Goliath fight, this time against a Russian heavyweight superstar to avenge the death of his one-time-nemesis-turned-lifelong friend, Apollo Creed. Rocky Balboa's son, now a grown man with his own demons, pleads with his father not to take the fight, "doesn't it bother you that people are making you out to be a joke?" Rocky shuts him down with a tough love speech that sounds so much like the truth that the cheering begins even now: "You're the best thing in my life" he says, turning the tables back on his son. "But until you start believing in yourself, you ain't gonna have a life."

This bit of pop wisdom brings us back to the turf of what's ours, what's God's, and what exactly it is that we have faith in. In today's culture, faith is now closely aligned with the self-esteem movement and expressed as confidence in the belief that we can be anything we want to be. When this is reinforced in the Church with a message that we are to have faith in our ability to do great things because that's what God wants—for us to be and do great things!—then we're back to the trap of striving and earning, and living in our favorite self-deception: "I Got This!"

If you're not quite seeing the problem of faith as a God-tinged form of self-help, consider this: in the U.S. alone, self-improvement is a $9.6 billion market of programs and products to help people live lives that look and feel more like they think happy, successful lives should look and feel. This market is so reliable that the self-help industry's best predictor is "the 18-month rule," (i.e., the person most likely to buy a self-help book is someone who bought one 18 months prior). Predictably, the life-changing Ten Steps or Five Ways or New Scientific Wisdom has failed to deliver and the reader is left to return to the well, still thirsting.[1]

Much like the corrupted papacy of Luther's day, the language of self-help (You can do it!) and the prosperity gospel (God wants you to be happy and rich!) has a chokehold on the gift of saving faith. Now, some good motivational language can be very helpful when it comes

---

[1] John 4:5-15

to efforts like losing weight, starting an exercise program, or completing a difficult course of study. Setting goals and rewarding yourself for accomplishing them is a good and often helpful human discipline. But when it comes to matters of salvation, we need to be abundantly clear: Jesus never says, "if you can dream it, you can do it!"[2] He also never says that the more money you give to the church, the more you'll be blessed (this is where the term *heresy* comes in handy). No, God's gift of faith is not faith in ourselves, our families, or our traditions, nor in science, reason, the universe, or karma, but faith in the one who says, "your faith has healed you; go in peace."[3]

The problem with this message is, you really only need the one book.

The great asymmetry

Our modern ears tend to hear the word "faith" as meaning the extent to which *we* believe. We see faith as something "we gotta have" and the more of it the better. Rare is the soul who does not, however, have days when they doubt some claim or aspect of their faith. This doubt will then typically lead us to question the reality of God and his promises, including whether or not Jesus Christ was really both human and divine, whether the churches are really working on His behalf, or if His death and resurrection was really, actually, in fact the most gracious bloody miracle in all of human history.

---

[2] Robert Schuller, from the book by the same name.
[3] Mark 5:34

Our doubting changes nothing. Because it is not really, actually, in fact *our* faith that saves us, but rather the perfect faithfulness of God. He began to teach us this lesson all the way back in Genesis, at first indirectly through His faithful relationships to Abel and Enoch and Noah, and then, ten-generations later through Noah's descendant Abram (Abraham),[4] through whom He clearly articulates the terms of His covenant of faith.

Of the many riches to come out of the Abrahamic narrative,[5] these simple reminders will help us realign ourselves to the truth of *faith alone*: Who initiates the relationship between God and Abram? God does. Who persists in faithfulness as Abram makes less than perfect choices? God does. Who bids a perfectly mortal and childless old man to "look up at the sky and count the stars," and then promises, "so shall your offspring be?"[6] God does. Into the deepest pain and longing of Abraham's life God infuses the promise of grace upon grace—a promise that any reasonable man would have considered impossible. But "Abram believed the Lord, and he credited it to him as righteousness."[7] In other words, Abram had perfectly imperfect human faith and that alone was enough for God.

We see this same refrain as the Old Testament comes to a close, and a restless world drifts between an ancient promise and the One that is to come. Through His

---

[4] Genesis 17:5
[5] Key sources: Genesis 12-21; Key NT references: Romans 4:1-3; Galatians 3:6-14 &29; Hebrews 11:8-22; James 2:23; Matthew 3:9; John 8:58.
[6] Genesis 15:5
[7] Genesis 15:6

prophet Zechariah, God calls to a people who were far from Him indeed, "They shall be my people, and I will be their God, in faithfulness and in righteousness."[8] This has all the tender devotion of a wedding vow, except for one thing: it's totally one sided, with all the promised faithfulness and righteousness being supplied by God. The people to whom God is speaking have lost all interest in being His children, and have not promised Him a thing in return.

We are no different. Jesus calls us before we know Him, and promises to be perfectly faithful on our behalf long before we even get what that means. When we begin to lose our way or our faith, He calls us back gently, patiently, and reminds us once again that He alone is the embodiment of perfect faithfulness. He alone was created to be both God and man. He alone dwells in the eternal intersection of the Venn diagram of God and us. He alone stands in the gap mediating on our behalf.

All we have to do is say, "I'm with Him."

Faith and the Rock

So how did we come to botch the meaning of faith and the right understanding of where our faith is to be placed? Well, seeds of the first radically divergent views are planted in a single word in the Gospel of Matthew. From this word—*petros*—and its varying interpretations, two distinct roots have laid claim to the Church, reinforcing

---

[8] Zechariah 8:8

two parallel identities about who we are and how God
moves through us from age to age.

When Jesus asks his disciples, "But who do you say
that I am?" Simon Peter answers:

> "You are the Messiah, the Son of the living God."
> And Jesus answered him, "Blessed are you, Simon son
> of Jonah! For flesh and blood has not revealed this to
> you, but my Father in heaven. And I tell you, you are
> Peter, and on this rock I will build my church, and the
> gates of Hades will not prevail against it.[9]

Peter—in Greek, *petros*—is the name Jesus gives to his
disciple Simon: on this there is no dispute. There is also
little dispute that Jesus is assigning Peter some level of
authority over (and responsibility for) what will become
the Church. Where there is grave disagreement is in what
Jesus meant by "this rock." Does he mean Peter *the man*,
an interpretation that the Roman Catholic Church uses to
support the legitimacy of the papal lineage? Does he
mean *the faith of* Peter, which is the common Protestant
understanding of Jesus's words? Or did Jesus mean *the
revelation of God* which informs Peter's confession that
Jesus is the Christ—the same revelation which awakens
the faith of every believer such that "All Christians are
Peters."[10]

None of us can say with certainty which meaning Jesus
intended since Scripture can be used to support all three
views. Which one is best? Well, just as it is in rock, paper,

---

[9] Matthew 16:16-18

[10] Luther, quoted in Lenski, 626.

scissors, each has its Achilles heel. If, for example, Jesus meant that the Church was to be built on *the man* Peter, then we're left to wonder why, among other things, Jesus needed to call and send Paul, who would go on to write the bulk of the New Testament as he preached and exhorted and admonished the early church on how to be the church. If Jesus meant that the Church was to be built on *the faith of* Peter—in other words, that *faith alone* is the foundation of authority in the church—then we need to ask how it is that many groups justify limitations on leadership roles according to education or gender.

If Jesus meant that Peter is given the new name *Petros* as the paradigm for how the *revelation of God* will build the Church—through people just like Peter—then what happens when churches fail to teach it that way? What happens when we forget to equip the faithful with the sure knowledge that the Church is built on the revelation of God *in each one of us*, and that the Builder is calling each one of us "like living stones [to] let yourselves be built into a spiritual house."[11] Peter gives further support for this idea when he tells the early faithful that, "you are a chosen people, a royal priesthood, a holy nation, God's special possession, that you may declare the praises of him who called you out of darkness into his wonderful light."[12]

This Scripture verse is the foundation for the doctrine known as The Priesthood of All Believers. "The royal priesthood" was once at the very heart of Luther's

---

[11] 1 Peter 2:5
[12] 1 Peter 2:9

reforms, but today few people have even heard of it. In fact, the original three identifying marks of the Reformation were actually 1) justification (salvation) by grace through faith 2) Scripture alone, and 3) The Priesthood of All Believers. But somewhere along the line we started doubling up on theological arguments over grace and faith, and pushed aside the part where God calls each of His children—not just church workers or monks or Jesus freaks but you and us and all to whom He has given faith—to be the "living stones" of His church. Just as it is with the *solas,* sin has gotten in the way, as pastors are disinclined to elevate the faithful to equal status, and the faithful are disinclined to want to do any more than show up for service, get a quick fix of God, and go home.

Which means that the people in the pews of the twenty-first-century Western Church are a long way from understanding that when Jesus rides into Jerusalem on a colt, and the crowds cry out "Hosanna!" and the religious authorities who felt most threatened want the crowds stopped, Jesus's response—"I tell you, if these were silent, the very stones would cry out!"[13]— is a wake-up call to us all.

When we shrink in the face of such "spiritual" talk, we miss the gift that is *faith alone.* Because Peter's life and witness are nothing if not a reminder of just how many ways a "living stone" can miss the mark. From trying to write his own version of the script for Jesus's ministry (to

---

[13] Luke 19:40

which Jesus shouted "get behind me, Satan"[14]), to
wanting to box the power of God into an earthly tent at
the Transfiguration,[15] to refusing to believe Jesus when
He prepared Peter for the ugly truth about his lack of
courage in witness,[16] to falling asleep in the Garden of
Gethsemane[17] (you just had the one job!), to thrice
denying he ever knew Jesus just after insisting he was
more faithful than all the others.[18]

What better way to show us that *we* don't have to be
perfect than to build His Church on/through someone
with such an imperfect track record? What better way to
reveal that, just as it was with Peter, we will inherit
whatever perfection we need through Jesus? On the
cornerstone of Christ and the rock that was Peter and the
living stones of our collective lives, God reveals the new
temple is the human person in all our brokenness.[19] When
we feel unworthy of such a call, that just means we're
finally getting it: we are saved by grace through the faith
of Jesus Christ alone.

Yeah, but faith *alone*?

Every battle has unintended consequences. When Luther
delivered his game-changing one-two punch—*sola gratia,
sola fide*—his intent was to save the people and the
Church from a lifeless faith. He believed that once "living

---

14 Matthew 16:23
15 Matthew 17:4
16 Matthew 26:34-35
17 Matthew 26:40, 43, 45
18 Matthew 26:69-75
19 N.T. Wright

faith took the place of this ignorant, doubting, dead "faith," the rule of Rome was doomed."[20] To accomplish this he hammered relentlessly and uncompromisingly on this single word—*sola*! His obsession was so intense that as he translated Latin Bibles into the vernacular German he actually added the word *alone* to this verse—"for we maintain that a person is justified by faith *alone* apart from the works of the law."[21] In this we see how religious fervor can easily lead a person to sinful overreach.

It took some time for the message of *faith alone* to sink in but eventually it did. Believers began to hear the Gospel in all its glorious freedom, troubled souls rediscovered the peace that passes all human understanding, and the Church began to take on a new life and spirit. Then slowly, inexorably, as it is with all human systems, a new culture began to take root. A culture that began to revel in the fact that it didn't have to do anything at all (Jesus said so!). A culture that was dead in a whole new way. Forget doing good deeds for all the wrong reasons, we suddenly had a Church doing no deeds because it didn't have to.

Luther contributed to this problem when he questioned the veracity of the epistle of James, which seemed to stand in direct opposition to Luther's message of *faith alone*. "For just as the body without the spirit is dead, so faith without works is also dead."[22] The conflict between Luther and James is rooted in how each man was hearing the word *works*. To Luther it was an

---

[20] Taylor, 493.
[21] Romans 3:28
[22] James 2:26

"earning" word, as in all the hoops the Church was demanding that people jump through to win salvation. To James it was a "responding" word, reflecting the fruit pouring forth from the life of a redeemed heart.

But the chinks in Luther's case were far greater than one conflicting verse. There is this from Galatians, "so let us not grow weary in doing what is right,"[23] and this from Philippians, "for it is God who is at work in you, enabling you both to will and to work for his good pleasure,"[24] and this from 1 Timothy, that we are "to be rich in good works, generous, and ready to share,"[25] and this from Matthew, "Bear fruit worthy of repentance,"[26] and this from John, "the one who believes in me will also do the works that I do."[27] And others still.

Even in the thick of doctrinal battle, Luther knew that faith looks very different on paper than in does in the flesh, where it is:

> a living, busy, active, mighty thing, this faith. It is impossible for it not to be doing good works incessantly. It does not ask whether good works are to be done, but before the question is asked, it has already done them, and is constantly doing them.[28]

Every great theological battle is shaped by the realities of its day. Although the "winner" of the battle is declared because enough people believe him to be "more right"

---

[23] Galatians 6:9
[24] Philippians 2:13
[25] 1 Timothy 6:18
[26] Matthew 3:8-9
[27] John 14:12
[28] Luther, *Luther's Works*, vol. 35, pg. 370. (LW 35, 370).

than his opponent, this doesn't mean that everything the opponent believes or teaches is wrong. Luther's *faith alone* message was a critical countermeasure to the corrupt Cathedral-funding culture of the sixteenth-century Roman Catholic Church but the truth of the matter is this: that world no longer exists. We no longer live against a backdrop of plagues and fleeting lifespans. In the age of modern medicine and life expectancies in the 80s, our daily anxiety is rarely rooted in the imminence of death or the fear of the afterlife but rather in how we are to live lives of meaning and purpose in the here and now.

Our anxiety is palpable. We are anxious because we want to understand who we are and why we're here—but when we look to ourselves or the fleeting creeds of the day for answers, our bodies reveal we're on shaky ground. We are anxious because we've taken God out of the picture and, as a result, are carrying around burdens we were never intended to bear (but still cling to our right to bear them). At its core, anxiety is simply "fear without faith,"[29] the truth of which is making itself known through alarming and unprecedented surges in anxiety worldwide.[30] Anxiety is the plague of the twenty-first-century, yet into this immediate suffering much of the Church still preaches the distant "prize" of Heaven. Why?

Have we forgotten that ours is not a "God of the dead, but of the living?"[31] Have we failed to understand that we, as living stones, are the stewards of the peace

---

[29] Kellemen, 10.
[30] Since 1980, reported anxiety disorders have increased over 1200%. Begley, 2012.
[31] Mark 12:27

that passes all human understanding? Is it possible that the lingering cry of *faith alone* is actually constraining His faithful, making pastors and teachers fearful of even hinting at our call to participate in the mission of Christ's church? When we teach salvation as nothing more than a good future promise that will make up for all the hard times now (not unlike retirement), we deny that our faith is a living thing—a "full-bodied response of trust and obedience"[32] which begins the moment the Father rouses us through the Spirit, "Sleeper, awake! Rise from the dead, and Christ will shine on you."[33]

This is the fullness of the Gospel our anxious and apathetic twenty-first-century world needs to hear: that each one of us has been molded and made for a unique purpose, that our lives are part of a much larger story, and that we are invited to heal and be healed as we grow into our true selves in Christ. Knowing the thieves of this world would try to rob us of every precious thing—peace, hope, joy, confidence—Jesus came down to bring us the gift of faith, "That [we] may have life, and have it abundantly."[34]

This gift is not a passcode to some posthumous bliss, but rather a timeless mystery that invites us all—today, this instant—into the immediacy of a life of "faith expressing itself through love."[35]

---

[32] Taylor, 488.
[33] Ephesians 5:14
[34] John 10:10
[35] Galatians 5:6b

For further discussion

1. Have you ever said, or has someone ever said to you, "have faith, things will work out," or something similar?

   a. What does it do to your faith if that "thing" doesn't work out? What about when it does?

   b. Would you describe your faith as steadfast and reliable, cautious and verifying, or selective and flexible?

2. Many people became Jesus followers (disciples) during His ministry on earth. However, the "12 Disciples" were the inner circle. They were with Jesus almost continuously for three years. READ Matthew 8:23-26, 14:28-31, 17:18-20, John 20:24-25. Describe the disciple's faith. Do you ever find that following Jesus is difficult?

   a. Now READ Matthew 6:25-34. Do you find yourself worrying or having little faith about similar things? What wisdom does Jesus give in these verses? Is it easy to follow His advice?

3. READ Zechariah 8:7-8. On pages 36-37 the authors give us the context of these important words from God. READ Lamentations 3:22-23 and Romans 3:3-4. What do these readings suggest about the faithfulness of God?

4. Compare your answers to questions 2 and 3 above. How would you compare and contrast human faith and God's faithfulness?

5. READ Ephesians 2:8-9. "Saved by Grace" is the verb or action, "through faith" is passive or receptive.

   a. Why is it important to understand the active and passive words?

   b. In light of what we have learned about grace (in the previous chapter) and human faith vs. God's faithfulness in this chapter, what is the apostle Paul explaining in these Ephesians verses?

6. On page 41 we read some descriptions of the ways Peter "misses the mark." What are they?

    a. Martin Luther asserted that "All Christians are Peters." In what ways are "All Christians Peters"? In what way are you a "Peter?"

    b. READ Ephesians 2:19-22 and 1 Peter 2:4-5, 9-10. What does it mean to be a "living stone?"

7. READ John 15:5 and Colossians 1:9-14. Luther tells us that we are "saved by *faith alone*" and also that faith is "a living, busy, active, mighty thing." In your own words, explain how these two scripture passages and Luther's statements are connected?

Scripture *alone*

In the long and glorious tradition of great boxing movies, the most heralded of all time—winning the Academy Award® for Best Picture, Best Actress, Best Director, and Best Supporting Actor—is *Million Dollar Baby*, the story of a 31-year-old woman from a long line of "trash"[1] who convinces a grizzled old boxing trainer to make her a champion. A great story is never neutral, nor is our response to it. Which is why people coming out of the same screening of *Million Dollar Baby* would describe it as very different things: a testament to overcoming the odds, or an action flick with a message, or an awesome girl power movie, or the story of a providential relationship through which two souls are redeemed, or just a really great drama. If asked whether there were religious themes in the movie, many would recall that there were some

[1] In the character's own words.

scenes in a church. Others might mention the struggle to determine whether euthanasia was a sin. A few (very few) would tell you that *Million Dollar Baby* was, in fact, a feast of Gospel imagery—e.g., a father figure giving his child a new name, *Mo Cuishle*, a name that would make her who she is to herself, to the world, and for all eternity, while never revealing until her final breath its meaning: "my darling, my blood."

In filmmaking, the director—in this case, Clint Eastwood—has the final say in how the elements work together to tell the story he's set out to tell. While making movies is a highly collaborative endeavor requiring the gifts, talents, and expertise of hundreds, sometimes thousands, of people, there is never a question about who the ultimate authority is. It is always the director. The Christian Church does not enjoy the same clarity. The question about who the keeper of the story is and who has the ultimate authority over how God's salvation story is shepherded is key to our understanding of the Reformation cry *sola scriptura*!

The story begins with the written source of our faith: Holy Scripture (the Old and New Testament) aka Scripture, aka *The Holy Bible*. The Bible is the timeless and inspired word of God's relationship with mankind and, for fifteen hundred years, the Church was the steward of its story. So what happens when the very people charged with the care of the Gospel allow the story to be rewritten with themselves in the lead role? God does what He's always done. He calls someone in to speak truth to power.

In 1517 that someone was Martin Luther. Seeing his Church so content to keep the faithful at arm's length from Scripture, Luther knew that the only way to get clean was to repent: to turn back to the source—the Bible—and place it, once again, in the position of ultimate authority. His goal was not to usurp the authority of the Magisterium (the Pope and bishops) but to remind them that Holy Scripture was the primary source of Christian life and teaching. That Scripture should direct the church and not the other way around. And that all believers should be able to read the Bible for themselves, in their own language and vernacular. This, he prayed, would not only ensure the faithful were right with God, but that the grand narrative of redemption would be returned to the people who, together as his "royal priesthood," would then share the responsibility for being the keepers of God's eternal story.

Sin and Scripture

Peter makes it clear. "No prophecy of scripture is a matter of one's own interpretation, because no prophecy ever came by human will, but men and women moved by the Holy Spirit spoke from God."[2] Or, as the Jewish tradition had long contended, "What God says, Scripture says."[3]

There are three primary ways that imperfect humans interact with this wholly perfect text. We are sincere in

---

[2] 2 Peter 1:20-21

[3] Schnabel, 34.

our love of God's word but sometimes err. We feign devotion to His word to gain wealth, power, respectability, or access, distorting the Gospel to meet our own ends. Or, we are so invested in our own idea of truth, we edit the Scriptures to tell a God-story we like better—or simply reject them outright.

Our best hope is to fall into the first category, where we will seek to know God's will through Scripture and sometimes come up short—either by lack of understanding or by our own sinful desires clouding our vision of the text. Jesus's brother, James, prepares us for this when he says, "not many of you should become teachers, my brothers and sisters, for you know that we who teach will be judged with greater strictness. For all of us make many mistakes."[4] Let's try to remember this whenever we claim we have the best understanding or are presented with insights to the sacred texts that greatly threaten our own sure views.

Peter speaks to the second category, warning us that there would be many who would "follow their licentious ways" and "in their greed they will exploit you with deceptive words."[5] We saw this duplicity from the get-go, as the apostles confronted false prophets who tried to steer the early house churches away from the truth of the Gospel to gain their own followings. This phenomenon is still alive and kicking today, filling amphitheaters with "the faithful" who are taught to believe that Jesus favors "us" over "them," and the only way to prove you're on

---

[4] James 3:1-2a
[5] 2 Peter 2:2-3

the winning team is to invest more time, money, and zeal in the showy froth and clamor of the Church. Sadly, this has become one of North American Christianity's "greatest exports."[6] We see this most often in nondenominational churches that are led by a single telegenic pastor (i.e., leaders who are not accountable to a larger ecclesiastical body). Without checks and balances, they "seem to be the most susceptible to this theological virus."[7]

Which brings us to editing Scripture, which has a long and checkered history. There was Marcion of Sinope, a first century leader in the Christian church, who couldn't reconcile (what he saw as) the judgmental God of Hebrew Scriptures with the merciful God of the New Covenant. To remedy this problem, he created a bible that left out the Old Testament entirely. Many churches still practice a form of this revisionist theology today. The thing is, when we lop off the foundation of the Judeo-Christian story we not only shed the hard parts, we make it impossible to understand the fullness of the Gospel.[8]

As it is in life, so it is in Scripture: there simply is no new without the old.

Thomas Jefferson would attempt another sort of radical revision: he simply took the New Testament and cut out all the miracles so that the Bible could now serve as a perfectly reasonable reference book for wisdom and

---

[6] Vanhoozer, 180.

[7] Ibid, 181.

[8] Although it is difficult to put exact numbers to it, the New Testament contains over 343 direct Old Testament quotations and 2,309 allusions and verbal parallels.

ethical behavior. For the modern mind that struggles so mightily with the supernatural (except, it seems, in the case of psychics, palm readers, phantoms, the occult, and UFOs), the *Jeffersonian Bible* is a tempting alternative. But a bible without the supernatural is not Holy Scripture, it's a Ted Talk®—peppered with insight but void of potent, life-giving mystery.

Truth and consequences

William Tynsdale was a sixteenth-century English scholar who was greatly inspired by Luther's commitment to translating the original Hebrew and Greek manuscripts into the vernacular language of the people. He skillfully and lovingly created the first English language Bible[9] and shortly thereafter was hanged (and then burned at the stake) for doing so. Luther, too, was willing to die a martyr's death over the primacy of *scripture alone* but ultimately the death he brought to bear was not his own but the bedrock of human confidence. As it happened, by denying that the Church was the ultimate authority over the Christian faith, Luther unwittingly planted the seeds for a new and totally subjective criterion for truth: "that which conscience is compelled to believe on reading Scripture."[10] When proclaiming these impassioned words, he failed to factor in that he was not the only person on the planet with a conscience and a Bible.

---

[9] The Tynsdale Bible would become the source material for much of the revered *King James Bible*.

[10] Popkin, 5.

Faster than you can say, "then he opened their minds so they could understand the scriptures,"[11] a whole new wave of reformers rose up. With the bar set at "Here I stand, may God help me, Amen,"[12] the idea of staying home and tidying up the Old Church's mess seemed far less inspired than forming one's own, with unique practices, doctrines, and lenses through which to view God's story. This morphing and spawning of newer, better, "truer" churches has been carrying on now for five hundred years with no end to the "inspired" variations in sight. So although *sola scriptura* had all the makings of a prophetic call to the Church—corrective, idealistic, hopeful, and deeply rooted in the Word of God—the wisdom of time has delivered a compelling blow: "the result of *sola scriptura* has been doctrinal chaos."[13]

How to trust a perfectly imperfect text

Once Luther asserted the authority of Scripture over the Church, it was only a matter of time before people started questioning the authority of Scripture (two hundred fifty years, give or take). Bold seventeenth- and eighteenth-century thinkers—many of whom were devout Christians—left the Reformation skirmishes in the dust to take up the great fight of their own era, the Enlightenment. Scientists helped lead the charge, building out rigorous experimentation, exploration, and teaching

---

[11] Luke 24:45
[12] Luther, LW 32, 113.
[13] Rose, 87.

programs that would later become the fields of study we call Anatomy, Biology, Chemistry, Mineralogy, Physics, and Zoology. Many in the Church celebrated the scientists' work as it unearthed the tools by which all future generations might understand the meticulous richness of Creation. But there was deep concern over the new standard-bearers' broader assertions. From here on in: "truth would be determined by what was observable and verifiable,"[14] the belief in a transcendent God acting in human history and revealing truth to people would no longer be the paradigm, and the Church would hereby be relieved of its presumptive authority.

This new "truth" should have rendered the Church extinct but it did not. Even after multiple generations of "old world" thinkers died off, and centuries of "enlightened" thinking guided the way, Christ's Church still thrived not only throughout Europe but Latin America, Asia, and Africa, as well. The faces changed but the truth of Scripture held its ground. Just as it was at the height of Christendom, today over a third of the world's population—over 2.3 billion people—confess Christ. By 2050 that number will likely be higher by a billion, with roughly 80% of the faithful being global people of color.[15]

This unfettered growth has only served to ratchet up the existential battle between Faith and Science, with scholars on both sides committed to undermining the credibility of the other, and disciples of each camp rooting loudly from the sidelines. Those who believe that

---

[14] Kloha, 2015.
[15] Jenkins, 2.

the truth of Scripture is obsolete will argue that the Bible is inconsistent with scientific and historic evidence. Those who believe that the truth of Scripture is eternal will oppose these persistent attacks with any number of factual assertions and scholarly insights. Here are a few we find helpful:

First off, *The Holy Bible* is neither a science nor a history book. It is the inspired account of God's saving relationship to mankind for all time. The issue of inerrancy—a stumbling block for many—can best be understood as such: "To say that the sacred Scriptures are inerrant is to say that their authors are absolutely truthful according to their intended purposes."[16] When we butt up against elements of the story that seem out of alignment with our modern understanding of the world, let's try to remember that we are just a blip in the timeline of human history: whatever "advanced knowledge" we think we have today may, a hundred years from now, be proven narrow, incomplete, or just plain wrong. The same holds true for the assertions of certain Christian groups at any moment in time.

Take for example, the belief in a literal six-day Creation. Throughout the entire history of the Christian faith, this was not a view that was emphasized or required. The Creation narrative was seen by some as literal and by others as metaphoric, with the word "day" representing great spans of time. Outliers, like the fourth-century church father Augustine, believed that Creation actually happened in an instant, and that the measure of a

---

[16] Voelz, 239.

"day" was God's way of unpacking for simple humans the various elements that were brought into being simultaneously. There was ample room under the Christian tent for all of these views.

Then came the Fundamentalists. Born in America in the late nineteenth- and early twentieth-centuries, this militant group emerged as a counterattack to the wave of liberal theology and culture in the U.S. In 1925, the Scopes Monkey Trial[17] would give the new movement their day in court as William Jennings Bryan attempted to make a case against evolution to prevent its teaching in public schools. The trial would be the nation's first live coast-to-coast broadcast on radio. The country was enrapt.

Although John Scopes lost the case, the Fundamentalists lost the battle for hearts and minds. While the chief reporting was seemingly biased, it did not help their cause that "Bryan's answers to [Clarence] Darrow's questions on the witness stand were embarrassingly naïve."[18] The Fundamentalists dug in their heels. By the 1950s they had created a church culture that required its members to deny all evolutionary possibilities, assert a literal six-day Creation, and separate itself from all dialogue and relationship with Catholics, the culture, and any in the Protestant tradition that did not stand with them on these self-declared shibboleths (tests) of the "true faithful." Because of their influence, many in the Western World—both inside the Church and out—now

---

[17] High school teacher John Scopes was charged with teaching evolution in a school district that forbade it.
[18] Olson, 564.

assume that a literal six-day Creation is an original truth claim of Christianity when in fact its insistence as orthodoxy is about as ancient as the pop-up toaster.

Another common sucker punch used in an attempt to disparage the Bible is that it's not sourced from "autographs" (i.e., original documents directly from the author's pen). This is true but not discrediting; in fact, quite the opposite. Because we don't have originals for *any* ancient texts—not from Plato or Aristotle or Homer or Socrates or Julius Caesar or any of the ancient writers and thinkers whose works sit unquestioned in the Western Canon. For example, the earliest manuscripts we have of Aristotle's are from 1400 years after he would have written them; there are 49 known copies in existence. Our earliest texts from Plato are from 1200 years after the fact; we have 7 of those. The collection of Homer is, by comparison, fresh and plentiful: 643 copies, the earliest of which were made only 500 years after his writings.

Which brings us to the New Testament. Thoughtful scholars continue to uncover and examine new texts, helping them date the bulk of the Gospel copies to within 40-80 years of the original autograph.[19] Many of them are eyewitness accounts, and some, like the epistle of James, were written and copied within 15 years of Jesus's death. So what sort of numbers are we talking about? Over 24,000 sources, including fragments, pages, writings and manuscripts. "There is simply no ancient manuscript in

---

[19] Middendorf, Lecture, 2012.

history that is more reliable than the New Testament scriptures."[20]

Now, because there are so many copies, there are also some inconsistencies among them. (This is also true of Shakespeare's plays which, strangely, we don't have any original autographs of either).[21] While detractors make a lot of noise about biblical inconsistencies, the truth is that 85% of them would be considered "typos" or the kind of errors one is likely to make if they're copying a document with a feather onto an animal skin by oil lamp without glasses.[22] The others "do not constitute major changes that affect meaning,"[23] or impact the truth claims of Scripture or the Nicene Creed. Examples of these inconsistencies can be found in copies of Romans 3. In Romans 3:22 some versions say "for all who believe" while others say "for all and upon all who believe"; in 3:26 some copies read "and the one who justified" others simply, "by justifying"; or in 3:28, earlier manuscripts read "we determine" and later manuscripts, "let us determine."[24] This is the nature of the textual variances in Scripture.

Which brings us to the challenges of translation and interpretation, of which there are two primary schools of thought. There are those who feel that the best way to do justice to Scripture is to use the scholarly gifts of theological, archaeological, historical, lexicographic, and

---

[20] Francisco, Lecture, 2017

[21] The New Oxford Annotated Bible, Essays, Textual Criticism, 460.

[22] Francisco, Lecture, 2017.

[23] Kloha, 2015.

[24] Ibid.

other academic training to expand our understanding. This includes contextual factors such as what was meant at the time the words were spoken, how a first-century Roman or Jew would have understood them, or why a certain image or metaphor might resonate beyond the surface of the words themselves. This is called "high criticism." These methods can be both blessing and curse, awakening new freedoms and possibilities for understanding, but also, at times, creating rifts with other elements of Scripture.

On the other hand, we have what is called "low criticism." Asserting, correctly, that the words of Scripture have been accurately and reliably transmitted to us over the centuries, these scholars hold to the literal definition of every word and phrase, with little added interpretation of any kind.[25] This view has been part of the Fundamentalist approach, and has a stronghold in many Evangelical and nondenominational circles today. Even in this small book, we've already bumped up against an example of the limitations of low criticism. Do we know what the word *rock* means literally? Yes. Does that tell us what Jesus meant when He said, "on this rock I will build my church"? Not so much.

Since both the high and low methods of interpretation are susceptible to the sin of man, how are we to know "the best" way to approach the Scriptures? Well, let's start with this: every person who picks up a Bible becomes—in that moment—an interpreter, bringing to the text "all that we are, with all of our experiences, culture, and prior

---

[25] Montgomery, Lecture, 2015.

understanding of words and ideas."[26] Mindful of this, our goal is not to be more clever or spiritually insightful than another believer, and it is certainly not to use the texts to support a given theological, political, or social view, but rather, simply, to get at "the plain meaning of the text."[27]

Still a bit confused? Well, maybe Luther's thoughts on translation will help put us in the right spirit to face the challenges of interpretation, as well:

> "What is the point in being unnecessarily rigid and cold in reproducing the words when they cannot be understood?" His formula was entirely intuitive: "If you can understand the Hebrew man speaking, then grasp that sense, and say to yourself, 'Now look here, how does a German say something like that?' Once he has the German words to serve the purpose, let him drop the Hebrew words and express the meaning freely in the best German he knows." The idea of free translation was so novel in the early sixteenth century that one is tempted to say Luther was centuries ahead of his time. The fact is, his intuitive grasp of language remains centuries, aeons removed from literal-minded scholarship of any age."[28]

In the beginning was the Word

"And the Word was with God, and the Word was God."[29] This is the truth which God spoke to the apostle

---

[26] Stuart & Fee, 18.

[27] Ibid,18.

[28] Haille, 69 from WA 38. See also LW 35, 214.

[29] John 1:1

John, gathering up all the words of Scripture into one unifying and eternal Word: Jesus Christ, God's word enfleshed.

How often do we stop to think about what a cosmic medium Scripture really is? Beyond the face value of a given verse on a page is the larger spiritual reality of how these words come to give us Life. It's a pattern that lives and breathes throughout all of Scripture. God speaks and new life begins. God inspires men and women to communicate words on His behalf and, embedded in those very words are the height and breadth and depth of the mysteries of the Living God. "Living and active,"[30] these words travel from person to person, century to century, continent to continent. From printed page to human heart, the Spirit moves from the soul of the first hearer who captured the words, through the transcribers and translators and printers and proclaimers who moved them forward, all the way to this moment, where someone, somewhere is hearing the Word for the very first time, with all the freshness of the first gasp.

This is why Luther saw Scripture as "the manger in which Christ lies."[31] He knew firsthand that it was a vibrant, wriggling, life-giving thing, and he wanted us to see it this way too. He longed for us to hear Christ calling through His word and to draw near, approaching with reverence, awe, joy, and great anticipation of the glory to come from the Word made flesh in our lives and in the world (fair warning: mangers are messy). When we heed

[30] Hebrews 4:12
[31] Luther, LW 35, 236.

this call, we join with the communion of saints who've wrestled in the muck with the challenges of their own era. Their study becomes our study. Their prayers our prayers. Their hope our hope. It is on their shoulders and through their witness that we now stand, looking through the eyes of Christ at a world that they will never know—and into which we are all now called to speak.

Together, may we join in the refrain: "your word is a lamp to my feet and a light to my path."[32]

---

[32] Psalm 119:105

For further discussion

1. Do you spend time reading Scripture on your own?

   a. When you come across something that is confusing or unclear or hard, where do you go for clarification?

2. Some forty authors, thirty in the Old Testament and ten in the New Testament, wrote the words of God that now come to us in our Bibles. READ 2 Peter 1:16-21. How did these authors come to write their portion of the Scriptures? Why do you think God would use so many different writers? What is the potential risk? What is the reward?

3. On page 63 the authors wrote, "Beyond the face value of a given verse on a page is the larger spiritual reality of how these words come to give us Life." Ours is a God of the living. His words are living and active.

   a. Open your bible to Genesis 1. How many times do you read the words "and God said/spoke" (or something similar)? What are God's words accomplishing here?

b. READ John 1:1-4, 14. In these verses the apostle John is explaining something very important about Jesus. What connection is he helping us make? What is John saying about God's living Word?

c. Theologians often say that Scripture is God's Word—Jesus—in words. What do these verses (in the table below) tell us about God's Word and words for our life?

Psalm 119:105; John 8:12	
Deuteronomy 8:3; John 6:33-35	
Deuteronomy 11:18-21; 2 Timothy 3:16-17	

4. In the previous question we learned about the foundational and life-giving importance of Scripture. On pages 54 the authors suggest some unintended consequences of Martin Luther's impassioned *scripture alone* claim. Was this new information for you? Did it surprise you?

a. How do you think these differing interpretations of Scripture affect the body of Christ or the Christian witness? Are there positive and negative outcomes?

b. Thinking about your own experience with consensus-building and compromise, how can we approach *scripture alone* (think back to the conflict over circumcision in Acts 15, and later, to the creedal process in Nicaea)? Also consider Acts 17:10-12.

5. Martin Luther said of Holy Scripture; "Here you will find the swaddling cloths and the manger in which Christ lies, and to which the angel points the shepherds [Luke 2:12]. Simple and lowly are these swaddling cloths, but dear is the treasure, Christ, who lies in them."[1] Why is this a good description?

a. What does this suggest about how we are to approach Scripture?

---

[1] Luther, LW 35, 236.

We *alone* are right

In the modern sport of boxing, the Marquess of Queensbury rules stipulate, among other things, the size of the ring, the number and duration of the rounds, and the fact "that each man shall be provided with a handkerchief of a colour suitable to his own fancy" (the combatant's handkerchiefs are then entwined to form the winner's trophy which is called "the colours"). It is also written that hitting below the belt, holding, pushing, tripping, biting or spitting are forbidden. There are four possible outcomes to a bout: a knock-out, a technical knock-out (not down but thoroughly debilitated), the highest total score of the judging panel, or a "no decision"—a pre-negotiated compromise to prevent fighters who remain standing until the end from being called losers.

A "no decision" is never a satisfying outcome for the fans. In fact, up through the twentieth century, the newspapermen covering such a fight would quickly pool their thoughts and declare their own winner—judges be damned. That's the thing about human beings: we don't like ties. We like winners. We like to know that at the end of a good fight an official will declare that one side was better (or, in the case of theology, more right). Pride, the essence of our sin natures, is always lurking just beneath our prayers.

We see this desire to defend our own superior positions in politics, social issues, education, parenting, and, of course, the best way to get down to our ideal fighting weight. When it comes, then, to the existential stakes of an entire belief system, is it really so hard to imagine that each of the thousands of different "denominational tribes" of Christianity are secretly hoping that when Jesus returns to gather up all His faithful He will pull their group aside and say, "Hey, FYI, you guys are the ones who really got what I was all about. Thanks."

We just can't help ourselves.

In the realm of *the three solas*, we see this arc clearly: the more people get involved the more things get messed up. Let's review our progression from *grace alone* to *faith alone* to *Scripture alone* to unpack this idea a bit more. With *grace alone*, the only lesson we need to learn is that it's all God. This may be hard to learn. We may wish it weren't true. We may even enter the Kingdom kicking and screaming and insisting we deserve at least partial credit—and maybe that's even part of the plan:

> If an unbeliever arrives at the house of salvation, he sees a sign on the door with two references, John 3:16[1] and Acts 16:30-31[2], informing him or her in no uncertain terms that one must believe in the Lord Christ to enter. An act of the will is demanded, and if it occurs, a person finds himself inside the house; he is saved. Then viewing the door from inside the house, the new believer learns from the Scriptures (if he or she is not already aware of it experientially) that what has occurred is not due to personal effort in any sense. The sign inside the house has John 1:12-13[3] on it as well as Ephesians 2:8-9[4].[5]

Once we have entered into the timeless mystery that all grace, mercy, power, authority, and love come from God, it's done. We're good. There is nothing more to discuss about how we got there or about *grace alone*.

Faith alone gets a bit trickier, calling into question the matter of participation. In other words, how we are to live from the moment of conversion until we depart this earthly life. In every church in every era for the past two thousand years, the pendulum has swung between a faith that requires nothing and a faith that requires something. The more we emphasize the nothing, the more a culture of self-focused, apathetic faith tends to takes root. The more we emphasize the something, the more people get

---

[1] "For God so loved the world, that he gave his only Son, that whoever believes in him should not perish but have eternal life."

[2] "Sirs, what must I do to be saved?" And they said, "Believe in the Lord Jesus, and you will be saved, you and your household."

[3] But to all who did receive him, who believed in his name, he gave the right to become children of God, who were born, not of blood nor of the will of the flesh nor of the will of man, but of God.

[4] For by grace you have been saved through faith. And this is not your own doing; it is the gift of God, not a result of works, so that no one may boast.

[5] Montgomery, 394.

caught back up in the vicious cycle of striving, comparing, judging, and despairing (will there be extra credit, God?).

Which brings us to *Scripture alone*. Oh, that God had recorded an audio version with commentaries and footnotes. "And what I mean by that is..." Still, "apart from the inspired Scriptures we have no other revelation of God, of His will, and of His redemptive acts in human history which can make us wise unto salvation."[6] This is where God has promised to reveal Himself to us and so we meet Him there, knowing that good and well-intentioned believers (and sometimes not so good and not so well-intentioned folks) will reach different conclusions about what the Bible says. When we, His servants, are tempted to think that it's our job to uproot "these weeds," let's remember Jesus's response: "No; for in gathering the weeds you would uproot the wheat along with them. Let both of them grow together until the harvest."[7]

What we believe

Visit any church website and you're sure to find a list of statements about what that church body believes. Oftentimes, the list will include why they believe it, articulating a clear Scriptural case for each doctrine. Denominational churches will typically post the views of their national governing body, while nondenominational churches will have their own informal creeds.

---

[6] CTCR, 3.
[7] Matthew 13:29-30a

But just because the website or church bulletin says *this is what we believe*, it does not mean that all or even most of the people who go to that church believe such things: *what we believe* may, in fact, be news to them. Because doctrinal statements are created by pastors, theologians and church leaders to maintain and preserve the identity of their denomination. They are made public in the spirit of disclosure, as well as pride in the rightness of their beliefs. Churches, on the other hand, are places where people show up and, if they feel welcomed and, moved by the Spirit, and, as long as no one says or does anything too strange or offensive, and the worship times are convenient, and the drive isn't too far, and they have something for the kids, they will call home. The only lay people who tend to really dig into theological nuances are battle-scarred church shoppers and aspiring clerics.

> If you were to ask the average member of any congregation to explain those (theological) differences, you would be apt to be met with a long, unpregnant silence. By and large they all believe pretty much the same things and are confused about the same things and keep their fingers crossed during the same parts of the Nicene Creed. However, it is not so much differences like these that keep the denominations apart as it is something more nearly approaching team spirit. Somebody from a long line of Congregationalists would no more consider crossing over to the Methodists than a Red Sox fan would consider rooting for the Mets.[8]

---

[8] Buechner, 2016.

If someone attends a church that baptizes babies, they likely realize that this is something "we believe in," but they probably couldn't tell you why. If their church serves communion every Sunday they come to see that this an important part of "what we believe," but as for whether or not it represents "the real presence" and what that actually means they probably couldn't say with any confidence. It is also likely that if they signed an agreement of membership, they did not understand the "terms and conditions" in the same way that the church professionals who wrote them do—not even close.

Using our own church synod as an example, a recent Pew Research Center study revealed that 68% of people who belong to LCMS churches today believe that "there is *more than* (italics ours) one true way to interpret the teachings of my religion."[9] This statement would stand in direct opposition to the Lutheran Confessions, which are the binding exposition of Holy Scripture as articulated in *The Book of Concord* (1580). This confession must be made by LCMS churches, pastors, called workers, registered service organizations, schools & universities, and others in leadership roles within the synod. Many gladly sign this binding confession *because* they believe there are no contradictions between *The Book of Concord* and Holy Scripture. But many within the LCMS, as well as the wider Lutheran community, maintain allegiance to the teachings of *The Book of Concord* only *insofar as* it agrees with their understanding of the Bible. In other words,

---

[9] Pew Research, 2008.

they believe Christian freedom gives them the right to hear from the Living God through his word directly and not through a mediating text. If there were to be a conflict between the two texts at some point in their life or ministry, they contend that Scripture should trump *The Book of Concord*. They believe this to be both biblical and utterly Lutheran.

If these sorts of intramural skirmishes make you want to run and find some other church or denomination where these things do not exist, we'll save you the trouble. This same sort of infighting exists in every theological tribe and nation. As this book is being written, the Southern Baptist Convention has come to blows over a key leader who called out members of his own denomination for sullying their Christian witness with political allegiances. The Methodists are on the verge of schism over the consecration of a female bishop—not because she's a woman, but because she's a homosexual married to another woman. The Catholic Church is in an ongoing tension between a Pope who wants to "open his arms a little wider" and a Magisterium that is prepared to fight all change at all costs. The Episcopal Church has stretched its tent poles so far that the seal on its churches' doors could mean almost anything. Yet another "new church" is battling problems of credibility and witness as its charismatic leader is felled publicly by his own sexual demons. And even the Universal Unitarians—an all-inclusive church with no fixed beliefs about God or doctrine—have come to fierce blows over an internal accusation of "patriarchy and white supremacy" among the predominantly white, educated, and liberal leadership.

The terms may be different, but the source is the same: pride. The sinful belief that we alone are right is so primal we convince ourselves that this is the "good fight" of Scripture.

It's not.

Why we fight

The amygdala is a grouping of nuclei broken into two almond-shaped parts at the base of the human brain. It is a God-given tool for storing memories, making decisions, and processing emotions—primarily negative ones. Fear is one of the primary conditioning agents of the amygdala. Most of us have felt it spring into action, flaring up at the base of our necks when we hear someone say or do something that appears to threaten "our way" of doing things. This can trigger our fight or flight response, leading to withdrawal or, more commonly in men, to aggression. The gift, which was likely intended to help people of a given tribe physically defend their families and villages against attack, often triggers disordered expressions of "protection" over matters of doctrine, practice and, in the case of the professional church worker, income source. In the twenty-first century, this can take the form of fighting age-old feuds, rejecting new expressions of faith, or battling opponents that no longer exist.

T.S. Eliot said, "the life of Protestantism depends on the survival of that against which it protests." If this is true then the future of the Church depends on our recognizing what we're fighting for, what we're fighting against, who we're fighting with, and maybe, above all, who we are ignoring while we're doing all this fighting. The *solas* can help us answer those key questions.

Take the word *alone*. The way in which the word is used in *grace alone, faith alone,* and *Scripture alone* serves two key purposes. 1) to establish what is essential—grace, faith, and Scripture—and 2) to declare someone else's teaching wrong. In the sixteenth century, that someone was the Roman Catholic Church which, by virtue of being the only church in town, was also the only possible opponent. Today the members of any Catholic Church in North America will participate at least as much in church and home bible studies as a member of any Protestant church. Any Catholic priest will acknowledge that we are saved "by grace through faith" and that Scripture is the authoritative source of Christian teaching. And far from the papal values reflected in Luther's era, the present day Pope Francis—who lives in a modest apartment and drives himself around in a Ford Focus—is wrestling with significant twenty-first-century theological, moral, and existential matters. For example, in a world that is becoming more global and technology-driven by the day how will we care for those being squeezed out by progress, or include all of God's broken children in the Church family, or respond when artificial intelligence begins to overtake humanity? If Reformation-era churches are still throwing punches over the wrongs of Wittenberg, they are sparring with ghosts. Even the good people of Wittenberg have moved on, recently launching a robot priest named BlessU-2 to engage tourists by dispensing blessings—a bold experiment in mission outreach through a partnership of local Evangelical[10] churches who desire to "become all things to all people so that by all possible means [they] might save some."[11]

Does that mean that there are no fights left to fight? No. But the biggest fight is not where you'd imagine it. It's not among theologians and scholars, or between Christianity and other religions, or even between the Church and the culture. The frontline is in the parish halls and pews of the local church, where the faithful have lost their hold on (or perhaps never even learned) the guiding principles of the *sola* truths, and how to embody them in such a way that they are empowered to live out their calls in the royal priesthood of the twenty-first century. Because the promise of the *solas* was not just about saving—but awakening—souls that they might play their part in the redeeming work of God. This is unlikely to happen until believers are clear on the essential and polemic aspects of grace, faith, and Scripture in today's world:

> 1) Grace is a gift from God alone both in spite of and in response to sin; *this must continue to stand over and against any claim that God's love and mercy can be earned or deserved.*

---

[10] This is the name for the Lutheran Church in Germany.
[11] 1 Corinthian 9:22

2) Faith is in Jesus Christ alone because He alone embodies perfect faithfulness; *this must stand over and against the modern use of the term i.e., faith in yourself, the universe, karma, or the modern creed "you just gotta have faith..." in which the object is left undefined.*

3) Scripture alone is God's living and eternal word for all mankind; *this must stand over and against claims that church tradition(s), humanism, science, ideology, atheism, other belief systems, or new insights have made Scripture obsolete.*

Each one of us could return to these truths daily as our restart button and never find them losing their punch. What's more, almost everyone in the Christian family would agree with them. The Roman Catholics. The Eastern Orthodox. The Presbyterians and Methodists and Adventists and Charismatics and Baptists and Coffee House Christians and, yes, even the Lutherans would agree. If the next exodus were underway, and we could only take one theological truth with us, the promise that we are saved by grace through faith in Jesus Christ alone as revealed through the sacred and eternal Scriptures is the Gospel truth we need to put in our pocket and carry around with us wherever we go. Just that.

Well, just that AND...

There's always an AND

We know it's all about Jesus; still, we just can't resist the primal desire to tattoo Him with our own church brand. So Presbyterians add AND the *Westminster Confession.* Pentecostals, AND the gift of tongues. Progressives, AND social justice. Episcopalians, AND *The Book of Common Prayer.* Eastern Orthodox, AND an icon-centric liturgy. Baptists, AND an individual's decision to believe.

It is the AND's that we fight over most fervently. Maybe that's because the AND's are tied, primarily, to practices—baptism, communion, worship styles, the role of women, the response to LGBTQ believers—all things that happen visibly, while we're all together in the sanctuary (and not in the theoretical brains of theologians).

None of these AND's impact even a dot or dash of the Nicene Creed—which the early church agreed was *all* we needed to agree on—yet we fight tooth and nail for the right to consider them essential. It's a losing battle. Because when we double down on our AND's, we do so to our detriment.

When we make Scripture the be-all-end-all and ignore the work of the Spirit—and vice versa—we create a deficiency. When we ignore the sacraments and heavy up on lively worship—and vice versa—our expressions of faith are incomplete. When we talk of love but never of sin—and vice versa—we have left the Cross behind. "When Christians ignore parts of their own message, it seems the Spirit always gets another group to emphasize it and spread it. Like flowing water, God always finds a way through."[12]

We know that God sees us as One church, but we just can't bring ourselves to act like it. Our worldview is too small, our trust too tepid, and our time—both hours in the day and years on earth—too short. So we fight to defend "the way we've always done things" or "to change the way it's always been" and don't even allow ourselves to imagine that the God who created heaven and earth might just know what He's doing in and through this diversity of belief and practice. As we speak, we might just be in the middle of a sweeping narrative arc through which all the shards are forming some transplendent stained glass window: who knows? What we do know is that these are our marching orders: "I appeal to you, brothers and sisters, in the name of our Lord Jesus Christ, that all of you agree with one another in what you say and that there be no divisions among you, but that you be perfectly united in mind and thought."[13]

So what happens when we attack other Christians? Well, like a cancer the damage spreads—and far beyond church walls. Because the world is watching and what it too often sees is a Church that fights with itself and everyone else. This, has become our public witness. And although the quantitative and qualitative evidence is overwhelming, few Christians want to hear it: the louder we shout in the public space about this issue or that in the

---

[12] Rohr, 2017.
[13] 1 Corinthians 1:10

name of Jesus, the more people reject the possibility that our God might be good or real or loving or theirs.

And the loser is...

Jesus calls us to be countercultural not combative. Which means the question each one of us needs to ask ourselves is this: are we willing to let Him subdue our sin-steeped desire to put our own preferences before the Great Commission?[14] Or are we determined to keep justifying our own "good fight" regardless of the consequences?

This is not a lofty or theoretical question. Because the impact of infighting hits closer to home than many of us realize. For example, how many Christian churches are there within 10 miles of your own? How many of them are growing? How much of your own church's efforts involve attracting new members? Struggling to keep the doors of any given church open means competing with all the other local churches for seekers in the same community. It's "a very competitive religious marketplace,"[15] with many people choosing other religions over Christianity—or, more likely—no religion at all.

According to new research from the Billy Graham Center, if the mainline Protestant Church continues their rate of decline they will only have twenty-three Easters

---

[14] "Go therefore and make disciples of all nations, baptizing them in the name of the Father and of the Son and of the Holy Spirit, teaching them to observe all that I have commanded you (Matthew 28:19-20).
[15] Pew Forum, 2008.

left.[16] Many correlate the reason for the decline to the mainline (more liberal) churches giving up the teachings of sin, the atonement, and the truth of the resurrection. But few evangelical (more conservative) churches have any reason to feel smug: the decline in the LCMS, for example, would put it on track to be shuttered even sooner.

"Survival of the fittest" is not a strategy that's compatible with the Gospel. If we're spending more time guarding walls than helping people find a way in, we need to face the fact that we've lost our way. We need to stop navel-gazing so we can see and know the people in our communities, many of whom are "sick and distraught, drunk, mad, melancholy, anguished, or simply bored to extinction."[17]

Congregations that are willing to hang up their gloves and think of themselves as "merely Christian" are finding new and innovative ways to share space, resources, fellowship, and mission—and discovering new life in Christ in the process. The possibilities are endless. But only when we're willing to loosen our grip on our AND's, and accept this undeniable reality:

We alone cannot possibly be right.

---

[16] Stetzer, 2017.
[17] Merton, 85.

For further discussion

1. Have you ever been so certain you were right, that you went to battle to defend your position?

   a. Did the other person appreciate your corrective action? Do you have any regrets about this interaction?

   b. There is a saying, "would you rather be right or reconciled." How do you feel about this statement?

2. The quote from Frederick Buechner on page 73 lets us laugh at the very human inclination to stick with our own church team. Have you seen this behavior among churches during your own faith journey?

   a. Does your church have a "what we believe" type of statement on its website or public documents? Have you ever stopped to reflect on this statement or statements?

3. C.S. Lewis suggests the journey to Christ is a bit like a hallway. "When you have reached your own room, be kind to those who have chosen different doors and to

those who are still in the hall. If they are wrong they need your prayers all the more; and if they are your enemies, then you are under orders to pray for them That is one of the rules common to the whole house." Reflect on people who are not part of your church, your denomination, your Christian faith, or any faith at all. How does Lewis's imagery help us?

4. On page 78 the authors write, "But the biggest fight is not where you'd imagine it."

   a. If you could suggest one thing Christians should let go of, and one that they should make a priority in "the good fight," what would you suggest?

5. Page 78-79 gives three short descriptions of how we can understand the truth of the *solas* in the 21st century. Is there anything you would add to these descriptions that would make it helpful for you?

Grace alone means_____ as opposed to _____.

Faith alone means_____ as opposed to _____.

Scripture alone means_____ as opposed _____.

6. The Nicene Creed was considered by its authors to be the essential principles of the Christian faith. Most church bodies still recite this creed today. We learned, on page 80, that everything denominations seem to fight about are not actually in the Nicene Creed (mostly they fight about the AND's). How has the Nicene Creed served God's church historically and how do you think it can serve the church and its members now and into the future?

7. READ John 13:34-35 (the great command) and Matthew 28:19-20 (the great commission). There are four important verbs Jesus gives us in these two texts. Describe what each of these might look like in practice.

Love	
Disciple	
Baptize	
Teach	

21st century man *alone*

"Once that bell rings you're on your own.
It's just you and the other guy." —Joe Louis

This is how modern man feels every day without Christ.
Through a perfect storm of individualism, secularism, and
technology, we have created an epidemic of loneliness. In
2004, when the most popular situation comedy of all
time—*Friends*—came to an end, 25% of Americans said
they had no close friend with whom to discuss important
matters.[1] Maybe this sad fact helped to fuel the popularity
of the neighborhood coffee house, and the notion of
"familial" ties to people you could count on "to be there
for you when it hasn't been your day, your week, your
month, or even your year."[2] As it happened, that very
same spring marked the launch of Facebook, setting off a

---

[1] Brooks, 2016.
[2] From the show's theme song.

tidal wave of social media "relationships." These new digital ties made it easier than ever for us to feel entertained and connected while simultaneously breeding our isolation. Today the neighborhood coffee house is as popular as ever—only now, it's filled with people who sit alone with their laptops, battling isolation by putting themselves in proximity to other people, who may or may not look up when they enter.

More than 44 million adults over the age of 45 now suffer from chronic loneliness.[3] Some suffer alone, including stay-at-home moms, empty nesters, the un- and underemployed, artists, immigrants, people of means, scientists, truckers, tech coders, introverts, the autistic and the homeless, the nightshift worker, the widow and the orphan and the prophets of God, and the many independent contractors, consultants, freelancers, and gig workers that a changing economy has given rise to. Some suffer in the middle of a busy day, surrounded by people at work—or even at home—while feeling little emotional connection or that deeper sense of being understood, loved, and cherished. Some suffer even as believers, never developing a true sense of belonging to a church body; or worse, having learned firsthand that brothers and sisters in Christ can wound and shun, opting out instead.

Loneliness in the final decades of life can be acute. To quell the pain, our oldest citizens are increasingly turning to technology. For less than a hundred dollars, a senior (or family member) can pick up A Joy for All Companion

---

[3] Edmondson, 2010.

Pet that responds to petting, hugging, and motion much like a real pet. In fact, seniors in nursing homes who were given these robot companions preferred them to an actual dog visitor. Why? Because the real dog could choose who it interacted with; the robot could be kept on the owner's lap and made to respond only to them.[4]

Sadly, our young people are experiencing the most loneliness of all. "Increasingly drawn to technologies that provide the illusion of companionship without the demands of relationship," millennials may be lonely not just from insufficient social interaction but also due to insufficient social *obligation*."[5] And here we begin to get to the heart of the matter.

The individualistic culture of the Western World and, in turn, our loneliness "is rooted in the attempt to deny the reality of human interdependence."[6] Do you remember learning in the first chapter about the *filioque*— the not-so minor revision that was made to the Nicene Creed? Do you recall that it was "someone" in the Western (i.e., Roman) region who decided to make a change to that fraternal contract? And that a whole lot of someones allowed the change to stand, quietly elevating the value of having their own way over the commitment to the group. Well, this embedded the sin of "going it alone" deep in the heart of the Western Church, which helped shape the Western Culture, which then went on to decide (naturally) to "go it alone," too. Which brings us to

---

[4] CNN.com, 2016.
[5] Turkle quoted in Beaton, "Solution," 2017.
[6] Slater quoted in Beaton, "Millennials," 2017.

the twenty-first-century Western World, where we are so successful in "going it alone" that we are literally making ourselves sick.

"Lonely people have more miserable lives and earlier deaths."[7] The state of loneliness alters brain function, decision-making, and the progression of dementia and Alzheimer's. Antisocial behavior becomes the default setting of the lonely, decreasing the likeliness of securing the very relationships that might help reverse their course. Lonely people suffer higher rates of stress, heart disease, stroke, depression, alcoholism, drug addiction, and suicide.[8] In fact, feeling lonely increases the risk of death by 26%.[9]

"Therefore, just as sin came into the world through one man, and death came through sin, and so death spread to all because all have sinned."[10] These immortal words of Scripture were spoken, ironically, to the people of Rome.

No man is an island

This line was made famous by the poet John Donne but its spirit originates in Scripture. "For, being ignorant of the righteousness that comes from God, and seeking to establish their own, they have not submitted to God's righteousness."[11]

---

[7] Cacioppo quoted in Edmonton, "Lonely," 2010.
[8] Cherry, 2016.
[9] Beaton, "Millennials," 2017.
[10] Romans 5:12
[11] Romans 10:3

We begin by asking what it means to be "ignorant" of the righteousness of God. Well, it does not mean that you have never heard of it, or never fully learned it, or even that you fail to understand it. No, to be ignorant actually comes from the act of *ignoring*. In other words, from ignoring the righteousness that comes from God alone. This is not a correction given to the world but rather to those who have been entrusted with the Gospel; namely, the Church but also the individual faithful to whom He has placed a sacred trust. Whenever these trusted ones choose to ignore His righteousness, they seek to establish their own.

The Greek word for "one's own" is *idios* (yes, as in idiot), which can be understood through the image of an island.[12] *Idios* is a choice, an identity, of being cut-off from the whole; separate, special, not like "all those other people." We imagine it like an island paradise, but in time we find ourselves disconnected. Bit by bit we lose our way, with nothing left to hold onto but our own preferences and our habitual reinforcement of them. When God throws us a lifeline (which, by the way, He does quite often—and not just to believers), we respond with, "oh, no, anything but that." This experience of choosing death over life is true for churches as well as the people inside and outside of them. In a culture shaped by having one's own way—by *idios*—we cannot help but share the same illness.

Make no mistake: loneliness is an illness. It not only doubles our risk of heart disease and fuels the decline of

---

[12] Middendorf, *Romans Lecture*, 2012.

our faculties, it also plays a significant role in the ravaging epidemic of opioid addiction which, in 2016 alone, led to over 50,000 overdoses, also called "deaths of despair." So too, last year, the CDC found that the rates of eight out of the ten leading causes of death had risen, reversing the rise in life expectancy.[13]

Loneliness is a sign that something is wrong. It is an aversive signal much like thirst, hunger, or pain. "Denying you feel lonely makes no more sense than denying you feel hunger...yet the very word 'lonely' carries a negative connotation, signaling social weakness, or an inability to stand on one's own."[14] In America, where we cling to the dual myths of bootstrap independence and salvific popularity, we surely can't go around admitting to anything as wimpy as being lonely.

Yet, like the deer that yearns for running streams, so the souls of millions are yearning for the life-giving relationships that come from the One who not only saves us eternally but heals our lonely hearts here and now. That's how He operates because that's who He is: a social being, a Holy Trinity who is forever interrelated and interdependent. Just as the Holy Spirit enlivens faith in the Son and the Son points us all to the Father and the Father calls His Spirit to move in and through our lives, drawing us back to Him through faith in the Son who seeks to hear and obey the will of God—and on and on—the Living God shows us all how to live together as wildly disparate children of the same Creator.

---

[13] Associated Press, 2016.
[14] Cacioppo quoted in Hafner, 2016.

Human beings are social creatures because we are made in the image of the Triune God. This is true no matter how much we deny it—that we're lonely, that we're His. Still, He calls us back to Himself and into relationship with one another, whispering that we are of infinite value (thank you, God) and just like everyone else (Nooooo!). That we each have a gift and a need, none better or more right than the other.

Awakened to this truth through faith, we are to have each other's backs. Not just the people we like, but all the beloved He brings together at the neighborhood church and beyond, including all the churches that confess salvation in Christ, as well as all the people who have never even entered a sanctuary, who remain apathetic or cynical or deeply distrustful of the God we love—by all means, yes, we are to stand with them, too, keeping them company on His behalf. "In Christ by faith and in neighbor by love."[15]

Communicating the love of God to a lonely (and often cynical) world is a very different challenge than the one Luther faced. To Luther's neighbors, God was a given; Christ was a given. They knew nothing about relativism, multi-culturalism, the internet, global input streams, Eastern philosophy, evolution, physics, hyper-sexuality, or whole blocks full of single parents and broken homes. But ours do. When they are disinclined or emotionally incapable of coming to us, the love of Christ compels us to go to them. And just like the disciples, we'll need to

---

[15] Luther, LW 31, 371.

travel light. Which means we just might need to put away our precious tomes and tells and church-centric programs and get back to basics.

Einstein knew full well that, "if you can't explain it to a six-year-old, you don't understand it yourself." So what if we made it just that simple? What if our lifelong discipleship process was simply to learn and live out and perpetually rediscover the truth as captured not in the words of man but in Holy Scripture:

> For by grace you have been saved through faith, and this is not your own doing; it is the gift of God—not the result of works, so that no one may boast. For we are what he has made us, created in Christ Jesus for good works, which God prepared beforehand to be our way of life.[16]

Any church filled with members who know what this verse means to the very core of their being—who can explain the implications of being saved by grace through faith *alone;* who get why it matters that we know we don't earn or deserve it; who understand we are not just saved *from* our sins but *for* a life of good purpose created in Christ Jesus; and, that God *alone* is the author of this great mystery which He reveals to us in Scripture—will be well equipped to travel outside of the safety of their sanctuary walls and into a world of loneliness and pain.

There, beneath a façade of anger and skepticism, they will find a deep and hidden longing for God that people

---

[16] Ephesians 2:8-10

simply cannot name on their own. They need the church to help. They need us to help. They need us to help assuage the loneliness that is killing them. They need us to be a friend—just that *alone*—and in doing so bring the love of God into the room, and maybe, in time, into the conversation, and in the process, renew our own depleted spirits.

We, the Church of the twenty-first century—as broken and lazy and stubborn and narrow and oblivious as we are—have been called to be the royal priests and mobile stewards of the tender mercies of God. We are like Joe Louis's motley crew reminding him that, even though he goes into the ring alone, we are there by his side—the manager and the cutman and the water boy and the gym rats and the sparring partners and the fans who cheer him on and who will still be there even after a crushing blow, just as we will surely be there to share those great and wondrous victories, too. Whether we like it or not— whether it's convenient or pleasant or beneficial or not— we the faithful are called to say to whoever God puts in our path, "won't you be my neighbor?"[17]

There must be something to it too, this church thing, because despite all the ways that we get it wrong, study after study confirms that highly religious people have far greater levels of wellbeing than do non-religious or even moderately religious people. Those who attend a church, temple, or mosque regularly experience a 30% reduction in depression, and a five-fold reduction in the likelihood

---

[17] Mr. Rogers, from the TV theme song of the same name.

of suicide.[18] We benefit from a boost to the immune system as well as a decrease in blood pressure.[19]

When a member is sick or struggling, another member will be there with soup and compassion. When we're facing an unfamiliar challenge, we find ourselves—suddenly—in close proximity to someone who has walked that same path before. When the world says we're too young to know much or too old to contribute, the church says come, bring your gifts to the table. And while it's true that being part of a church community tends to improve one's habits, outlook, beliefs, and sense of meaning, the single greatest determinant to this well-proven wellbeing is something even a six-year-old understands: you just have to show up. Even when you don't feel like it, even when you find the pastor's sermons too long, or that toddler keeps kicking the back of your pew unrestrained, or the coffee is weak and the donuts are dry, or the service is too late or too early, or the choir is just awful, or you're not even really sure if you agree with all this stuff, even then—you go.

And somehow things are better than you imagined. And you hear one good thing. And you make one person smile, which lifts your own spirit, and next thing you know you're spilling out into Sunday afternoon with a heart full of joy that needs somewhere to go and a whole neighborhood of lonely people. "And the word became flesh and blood and moved into the neighborhood."[20]

---

[18] VanderWeele, 2016.
[19] Luhrmann, 2013.
[20] John 1:14, *The Message Bible.*

We are not alone

Five hundred years ago, the truth of the *solas* helped to free the Gospel from a Church that had lost its way. We are wise to continue the good fight for clarity over the messages about grace, faith, and Scripture; wiser, still, to reclaim the doctrine of the Priesthood of All Believers which empowers each one of us to live out those truths.

To each era is given a new charge. The Ancients were assigned the task of disseminating the Gospel and discerning how the Old and New Covenants would be lived out together in practice. The Early Church was called to wrestle with complex ideas about the Trinity, salvation, and heresy, and to form a consensus about the true and orthodox beliefs of the Christian faith. The Reformation marked a historic call for the Church to repent and reclaim the primacy of grace, faith, and Scripture alone. The Enlightenment pushed men and women to use their God-given talents to explore the fullness of the universe He created, and test the bounds of His ongoing narrative in the world.

Who are we in His story? What is the role of His Church at this moment in time? In a world where nations stand divided, where people grow ever more alienated from each other and from God, and where our hearts are literally breaking from loneliness, maybe our job is simply to remind the world "that we belong to one another."[21] That we are not alone. That we are bound to each other

---

[21] Mother Theresa

by that One Great Love that unites us all for all time—even before we understand or believe the gracious and eternal reality of it all.

With hearts full of this binding truth, we give thanks to the communion of saints that came before us and will surely come after us. And in this the year 2017, ever mindful of our small and fleeting place in history, we honor and affirm the spirit of the Reformation by proclaiming:

Solus Christus! Christ Alone. *Soli Deo Gloria!* To God Alone be the Glory.

May this be our good fight now and forevermore.

For further discussion

1. In the opening pages of this chapter, you learned about people who are *alone*. Were you aware of the dramatic statistics detailed throughout pages 87-92?

    a. Has loneliness touched your life or the life of someone you know?

2. My brother's keeper. READ Genesis 4:1-10.

    a. According to vv. 3-5, what is the crux of the conflict?

    b. In v. 7 we see the first use of the word *sin* in Scripture. How is sin described and what are we to do about it? What do you think, "is right" according to God's words here?

    c. Imagine you are addressing your own child (or employee, sibling, co-worker, etc.). How would you respond to Cain's hyperbolic, and disrespectful words in v.9?

    d. What *is* the best answer to the question "am I my brother's keeper?" Why?

3. No man is an island. On page 93, the authors write, that "...we are to have each other's backs. Not just the people we like, but all the beloved He brings together at the neighborhood church and beyond, including all the churches that confess salvation in Christ, as well as all the people who have never even entered a sanctuary." READ 1 Corinthians 12:12-26.

    a. What is Paul trying to teach us by using this body image and metaphor?

    b. Paul pays special attention to particular attitudes within the group. In vv.14-20, what is the underlying human concern and what is Paul's correction for the church?

    c. In vv. 21-25, what is the underlying human concern (see v.21)? What are Paul's corrective measures?

    d. In society, who are the strong and who are the weak? How do we tend to treat these people? How does this compare to Paul's teaching about the body?

4. We are not alone. Consider your own neighborhood. Think about the people that live on either side or directly across from you.

   a. How many of these immediate neighbors do you know by name?

   b. What do you know about them?

   c. Are there neighbors who annoy you, who you kind of wish would move away? What does Paul's body imagery assert about your connection to these people?

   d. Now apply this same thinking to the people who come to your church.

   e. And then to the neighborhood where your church is located.

5. Brainstorm with your small group ways you and your church can be a solution to this epidemic of loneliness.

Bibliography

Alexander, T. D., & Rosner, B. S. (Eds.). (2000). *New Dictionary of Biblical Theology.* Downers Grove, IL: InterVarsity Press.

Associated, P. (2016, December 9). *A grim tally soars: More that 50,000 overdose deaths in US.* Retrieved May 2017, from www.statnews.com: https://www.statnews.com/2016/12/09/opoid-overdose-deaths-us/

Beaton, C. (2017, February 09). Why Millennials Are Lonely. *Forbes: Under 30*, p. electronic edition. Retrieved May 2017, from https://www.forbes.com/sites/carolinebeaton/2017/02/09/why-millennials-are-lonely/#257a581c7c35

Begley, S. (2012, July 13). *In the Age of Anxiety, are we all Mentally Ill?* Retrieved May 2017, from Reuters.com: http://www.reuters.com/article/us-usa-health-anxiety-idUSBRE86C07820120713

Brooks, D. (2016, Sept. 13). *The Avalanche of Distrust.* Retrieved 5 1, 2017, from NYTimes.com: https://www.nytimes.com/2016/09/13/opinion/the-avalanche-of-distrust.html

Buechner, F. (2016, November 4). *Denominations.* Retrieved May 2017, from www.frederickbuechner.com: http://www.frederickbuechner.com/quote-of-the-day/2016/11/4/denominations

Cherry, K. (2016, August 20). *Loneliness Can Be Contagious.* Retrieved May 2017, from www.verywell.com: https://www.verywell.com/loneliness-can-be-contagious-2795748

CNN. (2016, october 19). Robot pets offer real comfort. *www.cnn.com*, p. electronic edition. Retrieved May 2017, from http://www.cnn.com/2016/10/03/health/robot-pets-loneliness/

Commission on Theology and Church Relations (CTCR). (1995). *The Inspiration of Scripture.* St. Louis: Lutheran Church-Missouri Synod. Retrieved from http://www.iclnet.org/pub/resources/text/wittenberg/mosynod/web/inspiration.html#in-1e

Coogan, M. D. (Ed.). (2001). *The New Oxford Annotated Bible, Third Edition; New Revised Standard Version.* New York: Oxford University Press, Inc.

Cwirla, W. (n.d.). Believe it Your Way - Designer Religion in a Designer Age. *Lutheran Witness.*

Eckman. (2014, August 23). *Cultural Dysfunction in 21st-Century America.* Retrieved 2014, from Issues in Perspective: http://graceuniversity.edu/iip/2014/08/cultural-dysfunction-in-21st-century-america/

Edmondson, B. (2010, Nov./Dec.). All the Lonely People. *AARP The Magazine*, p. electronic edition. Retrieved May 2017, from http://www.aarp.org/personal-growth/transitions/info-09-2010/all_the_lonely_people.html

Edwards, W. (1888). *Art of Boxing and Science of Self-Defense, together with A Manual of Training.* New York: Excelsior Publishing House. Retrieved from http://www.nycsteampunk.com/bartitsu/manuals/Th eArtOfBoxingAndManualOfTraining1888.pdf

Fee, G. D., & Stuart, D. (2003). *How to Read the Bible for All its Worth.* Grand Rapids: Zondervan.

Francisco, A. (2017). Foundations of Apologetics. Irvine, CA: Concordia University Irvine.

Hafner, K. (2016, September 5). Researchers Confront an Epidemic of Lonliness. *NY Times*, p. electronic edition. Retrieved May 2017, from https://www.nytimes.com/2016/09/06/health/lonlin ess-aging-health-effects.html?_r=1

Haille, H. (1980). *Luther: An Experiment in Biography.* Princeton, NJ: Princeton University Press.

Jenkins, P. (2011). *The Next Christendom: The Coming of Global Christianity.* New York: Oxford University Press.

Kellemen, R. W. (2012). *Anxiety: Anatomy and Cure.* Phillipsburg: P & R Publishing.

Keller, K., & Keller, T. (2011). *The Meaning of Marriage: Facing the Complexities of Commitment with the Wisdom of God.* New York: Penguin Books.

Kloha, J. (2015, January 13). Commentary: 'News'week on the Bible. *Reporter Online*. St. Louis, MO, USA: The Lutheran Church - Missouri Synod. Retrieved from https://blogs.lcms.org/2015/commentary-newsweek-on-the-bible

Kolb, R., & J., W. T. (Eds.). (2000). *The Book of Concord*. Minneapolis: Fortress Press

Lenski, R. (1961). *The Interpretation of St. Matthew's Gospel*. Minneapolis, MN: Augsburg Publishing House.

Luhrmann, T. (2013, April 20). *The Benefits of Church*. Retrieved May 2017, from www.nytimes.com: http://www.nytimes.com/2013/04/21/opinion/sunday/luhrmann-why-going-to-church-is-good-for-you.html

Luther, M. (1999). *Luther's Works, Vol. 31: Career of the Reformer I*. (J. J. Pelikan, H. C. Oswald, & H. T. Lehmann, Eds.) Philadelphia, PA: Fortress Press.

Luther, M. (1999). *Luther's Works, Vol. 32: Career of the Reformer II*. (J. J. Pelikan, H. C. Oswald, & H. T. Lehmann, Eds.) Philadelphia: Fortress Press.

Luther, M. (1999). *Luther's Works, Vol. 35: Word and Sacrament I*. (J. J. Pelikan, H. C. Oswald, & H. T. Lehmann, Eds.) Philadelphia: Fortress Press.

Merton, T. (1983). Conjectures of a Guilty Bystander. In T. P. McDonnell (Ed.), *Blaze of Recognition, Through the Year with Thomas Merton: Daily Meditations* (p. 85). NYC: Doubleday & Company.

Middendorf, M. (2012). Lecture: Romans. *Romans, With an Introduction to Other Pauline Epistles.* Irvine, CA.

Montgomery, J. W. (2015, October 18). *Martin Luther's Stance Concerning the Holy Scrpitures.* Faith Lutheran Church, Capistrano Beach, CA, USA.

Montgomery, J. W. (October-December 1997). The Holy Spirit and the Defense of the Faith. *Bibliotheca Sacra 154* , 387-395.

Mueller, S. P. (2005). *Called to Believe, Teach, and Confess.* Eugene, Oregon: Wipf & Stock Publishers.

Oberman, H. (1992). *Luther: Man Between God and the Devil.* (E. Walliser-Scharzbart, Trans.) New York: Doubleday.

Olson, R. E. (1999). *The Story of Christian Theology.* Downers Grove: InterVarsity Press.

Pew Forum on Religion & Public Life. (2008). *U.S. Religious Landscape Survey, Religious Affiliation: Diverse and Dynamic.* Washington D.C.: Pew Research Center.

Popkin, R. H. (2003). *The History of Scepticism: From Savonarola to Bayle. Revised and expanded edition.* Oxford: Oxford University Press.

Robinson, S. J. (2004). Opening Up 1 Timothy. In *Opening Up Commentary* (p. 44). Leominster: Day One Publications.

Rohr, R. (2017, January 31). *Richard Rohr's Daily Meditations.* Retrieved from Center for Action and contemplation: https://cac.org/see-everything-judge-little-forgive-much-2017-01-31/

Rose, D. (2014). *The Protestant's Dilemma: How the Reformation's Shocking Consequences Point to the Truth of Catholicism.* San Diego, CA: Catholic Answers Press.

Schnabel, E. (2000). "Scripture". In T. D. Alexander, & B. S. Rosner, *New Dictionary of Biblical Theology* (pp. 34-43). Downers Grove, IL: InterVarsity Press.

Stetzer, E. (2017, April 28). If it doesn't stem its decline, mainline Protestantism has just 23 Easters left. *The Washington Post*, p. electronic edition. Retrieved from https://www.washingtonpost.com/news/acts-of-faith/wp/2017/04/28/if-it-doesnt-stem-its-decline-mainline-protestantism-has-just-23-easters-left/?utm_term=.e83b291ea465

Stott, J. R. (1970). *Christ the Controversialist: A Study in Some Essentials of Evangelical Religion.* Downers Grove, IL: InterVarsity.

Taylor, S. (2000). "Faith, Faithfulness". In T. Alexander, & B. Rosner, *New Dictionary of Biblical Theology* (pp. 487-493). Downers Grove, IL: InterVarsity Press.

Thiselton, A. C. (2006). *First Corinthians: A Shorter Exegetical and Pastoral Commentary.* Grand Rapids: William B. Eerdmans Publishing Company.

Towner, P. H. (2006). *The Letters to Timothy and Titus.* Grand Rapids: William B. Eerdmans Publishing Company.

VanderWeele, T. J. (2016, July 27). *People who go to church live longer. Here's why.* Retrieved May 2017, from https://health.spectator.co.uk: https://health.spectator.co.uk/people-who-go-to-church-live-longer-heres-why/

Vanhoozer, K. J. (2016). *Biblical Authority After Babel.* Grand Rapids, MI: Brazos Press.

Voelz, J. W. (2003). *What Does This Mean? Principles of Biblical Interpretation in the Post-Modern World.* Saint Louis: Concordia Publishing House.

Wright, N.T. (2009). *Simply Christian: Why Christianity Makes Sense.* San Francisco: Harper Collins.

Zoppelt, A. (2006). *The Word that Changed the World.* Retrieved April 2014, from http://www.therealchurch.com/articles/the_word_that_changed_the_world.html

Discussion Guide

Chapter 1 What's a sola?

1. Answers will vary.
    a. Answers will vary.
2. God makes several "I will" or commitment statements: make Abram blameless/complete; multiply (descendants); father of nations; fruitful; kings; everlasting covenant (for eternity); He will be the God of Abrahams descendants, nations, kings for eternity; He will give them land/the earth/ a home.

    God is requiring a visible sign, a reminder to the circumcised (and his spouse). Something they will carry with them always. It is a sign of confirmation, of submission, and affirmation. It is the visible sign of adoption into God's covenant family. Notice in v. 12 God designates this as an infant rite – like baptism – although converts of all ages are welcomed into the family too.

    God has made an eternal commitment to Abraham and all his descendants. Abraham's obligation is also eternal, it is not confined to Abraham and the present.

    This covenant is exceedingly important. It is a signal of inclusion in the family of God's people, it is a requirement (God commanded it), there does not seem to be any exception to this particular expectation. Failure to circumcise, is a breach (v.14) of the covenant and nullifies it.
    a. This was a sacred rite of inclusion that had been part of the identity and ceremony of the Jewish people for more than 1500 years. And it was commanded by God.
    b. Answers will vary.
3. Answers will vary.
    a. Answers will vary.
    b. Heresy—a self-chosen opinion. Anything that did not fit within the boundaries that the Nicene Creed was unacceptable or not considered part of the Christian faith.
4. "I believe in the Holy Spirit, who proceeds from the Father (*and the son*)." The "and the son" part was added by the believers in the

Roman See of the Great Church.

    a.   To the Eastern members of the church, this was many things; breach of an ecumenical agreement, a power grab, heresy, prejudice, bad theology, etc…

    b.   For the Roman See, these three words had become part of their liturgical tradition and practice for nearly 200 years. For those involved in the real-time conflict, this probably seemed like a part of the creed that had always been there. Furthermore, Rome had asserted its status as "first among equals" almost from the beginning of the church, e.g. we are the "leaders" and as such, we also have this power.

    c.   The heart of any philosophy that empowers us to assume the primacy of our own position over another's is sin.

5.   Answers will vary.

Chapter 2 Grace Alone

1.   Answers will vary.

2.   Pride, Lewis says, is self-conceit. This book asserts it is the claim "*we* are the god of our lives… we are entitled or deserving, and special." Luther called this "man turned in on himself."

    a.   Answers will vary.

    b.   Answers will vary.

    c.   Answers will vary.

3.   There is a saying, "Do not judge someone because they sin differently than you." Or perhaps this; "when one finger of blame is pointing away from you (accusing another), four are pointing back your way." St. Ignatius of Loyola might suggest starting every prayer time by first reflecting on your life as it measures up against the 10 Commandments. Luther's Small Catechism is a helpful guide to unpacking the extended meaning of each Commandment. Perhaps first asking God's help with our own sins would leave little time for focusing on the sins you perceive in others.

4.   Answers will vary.

    a.   If we are honest, we fail daily in more ways that we can even imagine – in our thoughts, words, and deeds. In what we have done and left undone. But God loves His very good creation. God saves us, through the blood of His son, every day, in spite of our failings. His mercies are new every morning (Lam. 3:22-23).

    b. Who will rescue me? In Romans 7:25 Paul answers his own question: Jesus Christ! Martin Luther calls this the "great exchange." In the greatest act of mercy and love, God exchanges our sinfulness and unrighteousness for Christ's sinlessness and righteousness. In other words, God saves us in and through His Son.

5.

Exodus 20:2	Gospel
Leviticus 19:2	Law, Guide (3rd use)
Isaiah 53:5	Gospel
Matthew 20:28	Gospel
Matthew 22:36-39	Law, both Mirror (2nd use) and Guide (3rd use)
John 3:16-17	Gospel
Romans 2:15	Law, Curb (1st use)
Romans 7:7-8	Law, Mirror (2nd use)

6. Answers will vary.

Chapter 3 Faith Alone

1. Answers will vary.
    a. Answers will vary.
    b. Steadfast and reliable – never wavering, never changing. Cautious and verifying – trust but verify, check the facts. Selective and flexible – open to new options, willing to select and accept new objects of faith.

2. In spite of their direct access to Jesus who was teaching, comforting, and encouraging them face to face, the Twelve were not always steadfast in their faith. Many times they stumbled, questioned, doubted.
    a. Jesus reminds us that worrying will do us no good. Our God cares for even the smallest and least of His Creation—He will not forget any of us.

3. God's faithfulness to His people, to His creation, is unshakable. In spite of our lack of consistent or deeply-rooted faith, God is reliable, steadfast, and filled with love and mercy. Faithfulness is not just a description of God's behavior – but also his character.

4. Faithfulness, according to one scholar, is defined as a "settled

disposition or character, " whereas faith is "a frame of mind." Our minds can change. God does not change—faithfulness is His settled disposition. Thank goodness for this distinction—what if your salvation was entirely dependent on your own human faith!

5.

    a.   One way to think about the Ephesians verse is in light of a nail and a hammer. Humans are the nail, we are by and large useless without something to help us. God is the hammer and the force or pounding blow is the faith he is giving us. God is active, and we are the blessed recipients of His saving mercy.

    b.   This is an all and nothing proposition – with God doing all and us doing nothing.

6.   You can also look at some of the biblical accounts cf. Luke 19:40; Matthew 16:23; Matthew 17:4; Matthew 26:34-35, 40, 43, 45.

    a.   We all have moments of greatness and moments of failure, victory and defeat, strength of faith and weakness.

    b.   Peter was called "the rock" by Jesus. Petros, in Greek, is a special bedrock type of stone. Notice in the Ephesians verses God's temple is built on a foundation of the Apostles and Prophets (such as Peter). Peter was a living stone. Peter then extends this description to all who believe. We are all living stones. Perhaps a bit rough on one side, smooth on the other. Imperfect and flawed. Useful for some things but of no use for others. Yet, in spite of ourselves we are all part of the building that is the church.

7.   Picture a grape vine . All the branches proceeding from the vine, the heart of the plant. Unless they are attached, they will never produce fruit. Branches that are broken or poorly connected cannot get the lifeforce necessary from the vine. Jesus is our giver of life, he nourishes us, invigorates us, through Him living water flows into us. Because of Him, we can bear good fruit. Fruit that is the good works that God himself has prepared in advance for us to do (Eph. 2:10). We can live useful lives, lives of purpose and calling, growing in the knowledge of God. Because people who follow Jesus will be changed people and the change will be noticeable.

Chapter 4 Scripture Alone

1. Answers will vary.
    a. Answers will vary.
2. Unlike other religious writings God used inspiration *not* dictation. God inspired each author to write the words that appear in Scripture. This is important because Scripture is not only reliable, but also accessible. Scriptures were recorded in the native languages (Hebrew, Aramaic, and Greek) of the authors and the communities they impacted. He used writers of every temperament, endowment, interest, purpose, perspective and even limitation. He used people that every generation could relate to. Some down sides? No two men will come at an event from the same lens. You may have noticed that while many of the same events are recorded by the different authors, these events are not always recorded in exactly the same way. Some critics would call these differences "errors." (In police work they call this corroboration. Conversely, if every witness has the exact same story it is called collusion). The up side? Since God wanted to reach all people, in every nation, all over the world, it was clearly and effective use of resource. On the other hand, some other religions argue that you can only read their texts in the original author's language. Because their god's words were dictated (not inspired). Thus translation into vernacular is not allowed. For Christians, we take heart because our God wants everyone to read and study and hear His words (think Pentecost). Indeed, our God is so big that imperfect people, years of time, and every language only serve as witness to His saving work.
3.
    a. There are eight creative acts spoken by God. When God speaks, something always happens! God spoke His creation and His creatures into existence. God's words give life.
    b. In the beginning was the Word—God's Word, speaking life into the universe. But notice the capital 'W' in Word. A proper noun – a name. In v. 2 this Word is called "He." In v. 14 this He is revealed as the "one and only Son" of God. In vv. 3-4 we see that Jesus was with God in the beginning, in creation. And that life comes through the Son of God. Jesus tells us He came that we may have life (Jn. 10:10).

c. Notice how Jesus is directly connected to each Old Testament description of God's word. Jesus, the Word of God, is the embodiment of each OT description.

Psalm 119:105; John 8:12	God's word lights our path. Jesus is this light. Light helps us see our way out of darkness. But we can also be light in a dark world.
Deuteronomy 8:3; John 6:33-35	God's word provides nourishment. When our souls hunger and thirst for nourishment, fulfillment, purpose, Jesus – the bread of life – can fill us.
Deuteronomy 11:18-21; 2 Timothy 3:16-17	God's word is light and nourishment. It is not simply some good moral teaching (although it is that for sure). But God's word is more. These are words to build a life on! (Mat. 7:24)

4. Answers will vary.

    a. One positive outcome: for those who care to thoughtfully dialogue and listen, consider and build consensus, these differing opinions can make us better—can help us understand scripture all the more clearly and meaningfully. One negative outcome: the splintering and infighting between believers over the smallest and sometimes most trivial differences.

    b. The 318 bishops at the Nicene council came together to discuss and debate. It was surely not easy to come to consensus, but they all sought accord, and all these faithful men relied on God for strength and guidance— humbling their own egos in service to the cause. In the Acts reading, the Bereans turned to scripture together. They worked together, studied together. It is easy for one lone person to read, in isolation, and "discover" something new, something that was never meant to be read into or out of scripture. Or hear some message that was not intended to be used this way. When we work together, we have more chance of success!

5. Holy Scriptures have been referred to as "God's Word in words." If you want to follow Jesus, you can find him in Scripture. If you want to know what God wants for your life, you can find out in

Scripture. Just go to the manger! But always remember... mangers are messy!

    a.   Scripture is more than a bunch of ancient words and stories, translated for our edification and enjoyment. Scripture is alive! It translates easily from language to language. Faith is awakened by hearing the word of God (Rom. 10). The gospel saves (1 Cor. 15). God's word is eternal, and useful, and living and active. (Ps. 119; 1 Tim. 3; Heb. 4).

Chapter 5 We alone are right

1.   Answers will vary.

    a.   Answers will vary.

    b.   There is companion phrase, about choosing which hill to die on. In other words, we all have to decide from one moment to the next, how important it is to insert ourselves, our opinions (even if we are correct), into the situation. Perhaps better to let someone learn for themselves. Or perhaps we are not as correct as we would like to think. Or perhaps there are just some underlying facts, something even of a personal nature, that we just can't know about a situation. And so perhaps humility is always the key.

2.   Sometimes we see this across different denominations. Even to the point of bloodshed. Sometimes we can even see this within denominations. For example: the more contemporary thinkers vs. the more traditional thinkers in a church body.

    a.   Answers will vary.

3.   What does it mean that we are "under orders" to pray for others? How easy is it to pray God's mercy on "them" or for your own ability to show love and compassion toward "the others"?

4.

    a.   Answers will vary.

5.   Answers will vary.

6.   Answers will vary.

7.   Answers will vary.

Chapter 6 21st Century man alone

1.   Answers will vary.

    a.   Answers will vary.

2.

a.   This appears to be a matter of the heart as it relates to worship. Abel brought his offering in faith, his "first fruits." Abel seems to have placed God first, his heart was grateful and he responded with thanks and praise. Cain, seems to have merely brought and done what was expected. Kind of like checking the box, maybe doing the bare minimum. Some have suggested Abel was God-centered and Cain was self-centered.

b.   Sin is crouching at the door. Think of it this way, Jesus is our Good Shepherd, simultaneously the gate and gate-keeper. If we choose to exit His protection, walk out the gate/door, exit the relationship – the communion with God – sin is waiting outside to nab us. 1 Pt. 5:8 explains that the enemy, the devil himself is lying in wait. In any case, we must resist what is wrong. All the while knowing our strength comes from the Lord (Ex. 15:2; 2 Th. 3:3). A Lord who says we will have trouble in the world, but take heart because He has overcome the world.

c.   Cain employs some hyperbole "am I my brother's keeper?" —he exaggerates his role as a means of defense for his behavior. Most parents (or bosses, or even siblings and co-workers) will see right through something like this. And after all, God already knows what Cain has done because, well, He's God.

d.   The answer is "Yes." Indeed we are all to do what is right by our brothers and sister (not only our brothers in Christ but in the world).

3.

a.   Bodies and body parts are all connected in very significant ways. We are connected via ligaments and vessels, bones and tissue, and you cannot just rip out or ignore some part of your physical body. And so it is with Christ's body of believers.

b.   Sometimes people feel like they do not have anything to give to the church. Or that their gifts are too meager, or maybe they are not educated enough or rich enough or (fill in the blank) enough. Or that maybe everyone needs to look the same or walk the same or talk the same. Anyone different is not welcome. But Paul reminds us that a body requires a diversity of members, of parts, in order to function. No gift is too small, no contribution unwelcome. Indeed some of the smallest, least visible gifts, make the greatest difference.

c. Sometimes it seems like the "stronger" members of a church can take over. They can exert influence through giving, or leadership, or volunteering, or bible knowledge, or just by being strong-willed and opinionated. Paul says, the "weaker" parts are actually to be honored and protected. Think of the spleen or pancreas, or even the brain. These are not the most beautiful body parts, and none can live outside the body (they are not tough enough for exposure), yet they are all imminently necessary.

d. Do you notice that celebrities, athletes and actors, the wealthy, the politically savvy, people who are in the lime-light, seem to be held up as pillars, icons, role-models. Yet, these same people are not as likely to be found in church (at least not in great numbers) as compared to the average Joe or the "least" of these. It seems that Paul would be disinclined to consider these strong and visible people any more important than anyone else.

4. Answers will vary.
5. Answers will vary.

THE NICENE CREED[1]

We believe in one God, the Father Almighty, maker of heaven and earth, of all things, seen and unseen.

And in one Lord, Jesus Christ, the only Son of God, begotten from the Father before all the ages, God from God, Light from Light, true God from true God, begotten, not made, of one Being with the Father, through whom all things were made. For us human beings and for our salvation he came down from the heavens, was incarnate of the Holy Spirit and the Virgin Mary, and became a human being. He was crucified for us under Pontius Pilate; he suffered death, and was buried. On the third day he rose again in accordance with the Scriptures; he ascended into the heavens and is seated at the right hand of the Father. He is coming again in glory to judge the living and the dead. There will be no end to his kingdom.

And in the Holy Spirit, the Lord and Life-giver, who proceeds from the Father [and the Son],[2] who with the Father and the Son is worshiped and glorified, who has spoken through the prophets.

In one holy, catholic, and apostolic church.

We acknowledge one baptism for the forgiveness of sins; we look for the resurrection of the dead and the life of the age to come. Amen.

---

[1] *The Book of Concord*, 22-23.
[2] The controversial addition referred to as the *filioque*.

OTHER BOOKS BY ICKTANK PRESS

Loaded Words™:
Freeing 12 Hard Bible Words from their Baggage

Man Turned in on Himself:
Understanding Sin in 21st-Century America

happy are those:
ancient wisdom for modern life

All books available on Amazon.

Made in the USA
San Bernardino, CA
03 October 2017